Heartfelt Acts for Teachers,
Students & Staff

BEST—

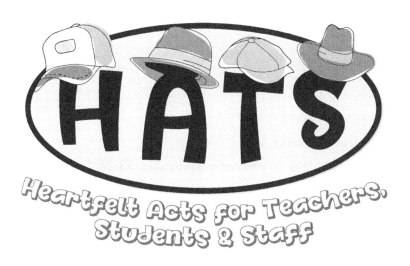

HATS

Heartfelt Acts for Teachers, Students & Staff

JAY BILLY, ANDREW MAROTTA, & BRIAN McCANN
FOREWORD BY BETH HOUF

INTRODUCTION

*"Before you can inspire with emotion, you must be
swamped with it yourself. Before you can move their tears,
your own must flow. To convince them,
you must, yourself, believe."*

—WINSTON CHURCHILL

I was on a Twitter chat with Jay Billy early one Saturday morning. The question came out to the participants, "What are some special things you do to inspire staff and students each day?" There were a lot of great answers—intentional actions by educators to brighten the spirits of their school communities. Jay answered that he wears different and crazy hats each morning as the buses arrive.

I knew Jay did this, and I'd seen pictures of his office. He described how the kids would go wild, and staff members got a kick out of it, too. When the chat ended, I began reflecting on all the great ideas that were shared and how I should and could do more. I felt inspired.

I thought more about Jay and the hats, and I could envision the joy and smiles on the kids' faces as they arrived at school. "How can I help get these ideas out to more schools and more educators?"

I thought to myself. I have ADD . . . It is a superpower, not a disability. My mind began to speed up . . . racing, thinking, churning like turbines in an engine.

HATS . . . wearing these hats was a really cool act by Jay, a heartfelt act . . . that students, staff, and teachers all like. *It hit me: HATS: Heartfelt Acts for Teachers, Students, and Staff* . . . It is the acronym for all of these nice ideas to help the culture, morale, and experience of schools and those who are in them.

Who could join us on this HATS crusade? Who did I know who is inspiring, creative, and not afraid to try *and do* acts of kindness to positively impact their school communities? Brian McCann jumped to the top of the list. He was a lifetime educator and leader from Joseph Case High in Massachusetts. His videos, enthusiasm, Positive Sign Thursdays, and more would fit right in! (And he's an English major from Boston College, with a master's in Journalism from University of Michigan, so he could help clean up my and Jay's mess of writings).

BAM! The idea of HATS was born, and off we went. It is our true hope you enjoy these stories, experiences, and heartfelt acts. Take them and use them at your school. You don't need permission, training, or a title. You just have to roll your sleeves up and get to it.

You can read the chapters from start to finish in order or sprinkle around, a little here, a little there. You can read one excerpt and put it into action tomorrow. We are excited for you and grateful to you for reading our book.

We are also thankful to our guest participants for sharing their stories and their heartfelt acts in the book. Each is unique and special. We appreciate them writing down their special gifts and acts from around the country with us in HATS:

Introduction

Lindsay Allen (Kentucky), Michael C. Brown (Maryland), Martin Geoghegan (Massachusetts), Casey Hallgarth (Oregon), Heather Heidelberg (New York), Mindy Milavsky (New Jersey), Jeanne Muzi (New Jersey), Meaghan Redmond (Alaska), Cassie Rodriguez (New York), Kevin Spainhour (North Carolina), Jessica Stokes (Pennsylvania), Christopher Turnbull (New Jersey), Austin Wilson (New York).

There is no perfect recipe, no perfect order for these HATS. Take them and make them yours in your own special way at your school and beyond. Keep rolling on your journey. #HATS

—Andrew Marotta

FOREWORD

—BETH HOUF

My mission as a building principal has always been to build a culture that has students, staff, and families running to the school and not out. How does a school principal do this? First, building a foundation of trust. Students and staff must feel safe and that they belong. Diversity should be honored and celebrated to bring a school together instead of separating or building silos. Building a positive school culture is a never-ending goal. It must be a continual focus of the building leader and all stakeholders in the school. This work is not easy, nor for the faint of heart. I tried to do it all alone when I began my journey as a brand-new school principal. I failed miserably. I contemplated leaving the field of education and had my sights set on returning to school to be a nurse. Then, a colleague of mine encouraged me to go to a national principal conference in Nashville. It was one of the best decisions I have ever made.

At the conference, we met principals from all over the country who were dealing with similar concerns that I had. Sitting and talking together helped me understand that this was what I was missing . . . support. At this moment, my PLN (professional learning network) began. Jay Billy was one of the principals in this group. As we were talking, he asked me if I was on Twitter. I rolled my eyes. I had no desire to open myself up to one.more.social.media. site. He told me I was missing out on 24/7 professional development and connecting to other school leaders. I was skeptical, but then he showed me exactly how to use this new tool that would be life changing.

I returned to school the following fall, with transforming school culture at the heart of our school improvement plan. I learned that when you lead with culture, the data moves more quickly in a positive direction.

Becoming a connected educator led me to meet Dave and Shelley Burgess. Fast forward a couple of years, and Shelley and I co-authored the book *Lead Like a PIRATE; Make Your School Amazing For Students & Staff*, as well as built a strong network through our weekly Twitter chats centered on school leadership. These chats led me to both Brian McCann and Andrew Marotta. Jay, Brian, and Andrew are examples of sustaining a focus on culture in a school building. Each of them provides inspiration and motivation not only to me but to educators across the globe. From the moment you step into a room with any of them, you can feel the positive energy and passion.

The collaboration of Jay, Brian, and Andrew has led to a book of pure inspiration, motivation, and action-oriented ideas. Through each page of *HATS: Heartfelt Acts for Teachers, Students & Staff*, they remind us of the most important thing about school . . . the people. These heartfelt acts will give you ideas for your school and hopefully help you remember the amazing things you are already doing as an educator. Don't forget to tell your stories. You never know whom you might be inspiring. Thank you to Jay, Brian, and Andrew for your daily impact on our world for the better.

Beth Houf is the principal of Capital City High School in the Jefferson City (Missouri) School District. Beth is the co-author of **Lead Like A Pirate: Making School Amazing for Your Students and Staff** *as well as a national presenter and student advocate. In her prior role as principal of Fulton Middle School in Central Missouri, Beth was honored in 2019 as an NASSP National Digital Principal of the Year and in 2021 as Missouri's Middle School Principal of the Year. In 2022, Beth Houf was named National Principal of the Year by the National Association of Secondary School Principals.*

Dedication

We dedicate this book to all of the hardworking, dedicated, and inspirational teachers, professional staff, and administrators in our schools, in our country, and around the world. You are the true heroes. It is you, with your caring hearts and creative minds, who make schools so memorable and special.

This book is a tribute to all the HATS you make happen each and every day. Thank you. We wish you the best on your journey.

TABLE OF CONTENTS

Table of Contents

CHAPTER 1

HATS IN ACTION

Wearing HATs

Jay Billy

Each morning when students arrive, I greet them while I'm wearing a hat. I own about 100 different hats. Some are baseball hats, some are fedoras, some are beanies, some are silly, and some represent different animals or food groups. The funny thing is . . . I'm not a hat guy and seldom wear a hat in my "real" life, despite my bald head. So why is wearing a hat each morning so important to me and our school culture?

One morning, many years ago, as I was greeting students arriving on the buses, a student came up to me and gave me a hat. It was a simple baseball hat with a Superman logo on it. This student knew that I was a Superman fan, and it was kind of him to give this to me. The next day as buses arrived, I was wearing the hat that he had given to me. It brought such a smile to his face and to the faces of many other students that it made me think about how I greeted kids on a daily basis. When kids come to school looking forward to the day and to those special moments, we have a really good chance of keeping their engagement and enthusiasm for learning.

From that time on, I began accumulating and wearing hats out for arrival and dismissal. Students often pull up to school in the morning wanting to see what I have on. They laugh or giggle when I wear a Pizza Hat, or a Tie-Dye big hat, or just a simple hat that one of them may have given me. Some mornings, when it's so hectic and I might be running behind, I forget to put a hat on. Invariably, the first students who get off the bus or even the bus drivers will ask, "Where's your hat today?" It has just become my "Thing."

One morning, I was out welcoming the buses, and a parent came up to me to give me a hat. He explained that this hat was from his mother, who lives far away on a Caribbean island, and she'd made it for me because she was so grateful for the weekly newsletters, where I highlight what is going on in school and often share pictures from the lessons and classrooms. Because she lives so far away, it gives her an opportunity to see her grandson and see what he is up to. This hat is woven out of palm leaves into a fedora-type hat, and it is my favorite hat of all time. It signifies what I do, why I do it, and who I'm doing it for.

Putting on this HAT: Whether you know it or not, the kids and the grown-ups are watching you. The littlest thing that you do could make their day. When I first wore a hat, it made one student's day. When I wear a hat every day, it brings a smile to many faces as they pull up to the school. It takes very little effort, but the effects could be remembered for a long time. Recently, a new administrator for our district drove by one morning and saw me out greeting kids with my hat on. She saw me with a different hat the next day and the next day . . . She reached out to let me know how really special it was that I met our students each day like that, and she could feel the joy in their arrival. Wearing different hats makes our school a special place.

Gentling
Andrew Marotta

I have been a foot-on-the-pedal, full-speed-ahead person for much of my life. Always pushing harder, stronger, and faster. "Alotta Marotta" is my nickname. This trait has helped me in many situations. Getting my first teaching job, marrying my wife, becoming an NCAA Men's Division One College Basketball referee, and more. I achieved many of these things because I pushed. Pushed hard.

As I have gotten older, I have learned that this way isn't the only way. Not every nail needs a hammer. My wife, Jennifer, has also helped me understand this concept. She is a guidance counselor in an elementary school close to our home.

We recently watched *60 Minutes* together. I've always enjoyed watching this show, even as a kid with my folks. The episode was about a prison in Wyoming that trained wild horses and then put them up for adoption. The inmates trained the horses. They went on to explain that the training benefited not only the horses but even more so the inmates.

They do not use the old-fashioned way of "breaking" a horse. They use a process called "gentling." Just like it sounds, they do not use force. The inmates and trainers use a combination of patience, persistence, and an even keel. They control their emotions, and, in turn, they can control the horse's emotions and behavior.

Putting on this HAT: When the CBS News reporter used the word "gentling," my wife and I both sat up a little and locked eyes. She knew I had heard it, and we smiled. We continued watching as the inmate, almost Jedi-like, held his hand out, palm down, toward the 1000-pound horse, and slowly approached. He walked ever so slowly, and eventually put his hand on the horse's neck, the first-ever human touch. He went on to pet the horse on the neck, back, and hindquarters.

You can view the full episode here: https://bit.ly/ELBGentling

Be gentle with staff and students. We do not know what they are going through. We don't know their full history or, in the moment, what is happening. Gentleness, kindness, and grace will carry you much further along in life, and your staff and students will appreciate you more. While my wife has not had to hold her hand out, palm down, and, Jedi-like, train me,  she, along with many wise mentors and family, have shown me the power of gentling and showing kindness, persistence, and grace.

Be gentle with others. This can be a beautiful HAT.

Dancing with the Teachers
Brian McCann

I'd like to think instead of "stealing" an idea from another school, I had been "inspired" instead to make it my own.

I was on a multi-day accreditation event when a group of educators from the team debriefed at the end of a long evaluative day. The subject of raising money in school came up. I spoke about how we had put together a tongue-in-cheek beauty pageant called "Mr.

Joseph Case High School" that had generated enough money to fund smaller clubs that really don't have any avenue to raise monies outside of blatantly selling things.

I will talk more about Mr. Joseph Case High School later in this chapter.

One urban school administrator boasted how popular and profitable the school's Dancing with the Teachers event was, modeled after the popular show that pairs professional dancers with celebrities whose terpsichorean talents run the gamut.

Inspired (but perhaps thieved), I brought the idea back to my school to our drama director, who had recently started a dance team at the school.

What a perfect way to spotlight a new club, raise interest, and make enough money for the club to compete in interscholastic events for the rest of the school year.

We found a Thursday evening in the dead of winter, to avoid conflict with previously scheduled sports games. Members of the dance team sought educators in the building to partner with them for a three- to five-minute dance in the style of their choice. Student invitations to teachers became like prom season: who had asked who to the event, and what were the reverberations because of this partnership?

About ten couples participated in this pilot competition. People rehearsed throughout the building after school during the weeks that led up to the event. Each group was in charge of its routine, the costuming, as well as any necessary props.

Even the principal was asked. Flattered, I agreed. I'm not sure if the young lady knew the exact extent of my dancing limitations. She wanted to win the event. I just didn't want to embarrass myself too badly. I was part of a two-person dancing ABBA tribute. I just hoped my "Dancing Queen" crown wasn't tarnished after the evening.

I'll spare you the highs, lows, and general fear that pervaded me in the week leading up to it. I was successful in the fact that I got through the routine without mistakes, and I smiled the whole time. My partner was fabulous, and I got to know this student a lot better during rehearsals and performances.

We didn't win, by the way. A tap-dancing twenty-some math teacher won. She and her partner were indeed great. They awarded me a consolation medal I hung in my office for years.

The dance company raised lots of money that evening. They never had to worry about paying any bill that year. The auditorium was packed with students, teachers, families, and community members who repeatedly told me that this was one of their favorite nights at the high school in recent memory.

And it really didn't cost me anything—except for a few tears of pride.

Fast-forward a few years, and Dancing with the Teachers is now an annual event. It has grown in participation to include teachers from the middle school. Last year, the varsity basketball coach gave us all a run for our money. The cheers from the audience were deafening that night.

Most importantly, it was a chance for a community to gather, to celebrate, to laugh *together*.

Putting on this HAT: Inspired by a school situated hours from my town, the high school took a big risk in piloting this event. Hats off to those students in Year #1 and their educator partners who believed in the possibility of fun for one school night. The monies raised do not come close to representing the joy this event has brought the school year after year.

I danced for two years with my original partner. When she graduated, her sister asked me to partner during her sophomore year. How could I say no? I swallowed my pride and prayed I wouldn't embarrass myself *this* year.

We came in second!

Popsicles on the Playground
Jay Billy

If you're a passionate school leader, you often get your energy from your interactions with students. I know that, when I can spend time with kids, I feel like I'm making a difference. You also know that summer, although a time for rest and relaxation, is also a time when you have many fewer opportunities to interact with students. Less time with students often makes for a boring summer. We work on planning for the new school year. We make schedules, plan events, and clean everything—but we still miss the kids.

That's where "Popsicles on the Playground" comes in. Although a scheduled activity is fun, I also enjoy spontaneous events. Think about this! I'm sitting at my desk, and I notice it's going to be a beautiful evening. I'm itching to see some kids and reenergize those connections that give me the reasons for doing what I do. I check the weather, and it's going to be nice tonight and tomorrow night. Then I send out a quick email inviting all families to come join me for Popsicles on the Playground. That's it. I go out and purchase enough popsicles/ice pops for about 150–200 kids, and then I wait.

For our new families, this is an opportunity to meet other parents and for their children to meet other children in our school. For our families who have been part of our "School Family," this is an opportunity for them to get out for the night and entertain their children without much fuss. The relaxed atmosphere and "no expectations" event allow everyone to feel at home, which is what I want our school to be. The kids come and play; the parents talk and socialize. For those who can't make it . . . No big deal. They didn't even have to tell their children that it was happening.

Over the years, Popsicles on the Playground has given me the opportunity to connect with new students and their families, reconnect with familiar students and families, and give me the boost I need to finish all of my summer duties and get primed for the new school year.

For the kids, it is a fun night out, away from the TV, and it reminds them that school is just around the corner and that school is where all of the fun things happen. Oftentimes some of the staff will show up, giving them the passion/push for the new school year as well. If staff have children, then it allows them an even deeper connection to our school family by including them in these events.

Putting on this HAT: Sometimes it's as simple as just making a time and a place for people to show up and just be together. Whether kids or parents know it or not, they miss the structure of school during the summer and enjoy seeing friends in a different setting. I often think about how events like these can be brought to the secondary level. Little cost, not a lot of planning, but some real connection time with families and students. The ideas include semi-spontaneous things like:

- Gather a team and join us for a kickball tournament against staff.

- Meetups at local businesses like ice cream shops or pizza parlors (warn the owners ahead of time).

- Meet up on the sports field for night softball.

Whatever you choose to incorporate into your school culture, you are bringing students and families together in a positive way.

National Anthem
Brian McCann

Unified Sports are some of my favorite activities at the high school. Not only do I love to see our special-ed students collaborating with their school peers on the court and field, but I love to see the happiness that it brings to all those who bear witness to these events. If you want to know what sheer joy in school looks like, attend a Unified Sporting event.

I was in the gym after school one day for the first Unified Basketball game of the season. Attendance was pretty good, but I especially noticed a strong showing from the varsity football team, who were dismissed from practice early to support the Unified Basketball players. The energy was high in the gym that afternoon, especially at the start of the game, when all of the players on both sides were introduced by name.

The game was about to begin when I asked about the national anthem. The game announcers could not find the connection to link the speakers to the music system, so they were going to forego the anthem.

I asked them to hand me the microphone.

I cleared my throat, asked the crowd to stand, and started on the lowest note I could find in my register.

And I prayed that I would remember the correct words.

"The Star-Spangled Banner" is not an easy song to sing. It encompasses a huge range of notes and is so well-known that any misstep is instantly identifiable.

Yes, the high-school principal sang the national anthem at the Unified Basketball opener that year. I remembered all the words (and for those with a music background, remained in the same key without modulating the verse *"And the rockets' red glare . . .").*

The crowd faced the flag and were reverent. No snickers. No muffled laughs.

It might not have been pretty, but I made it through without cracking or stumbling. I was greeted by enthusiastic applause, but the spotlight quickly returned to the players.

A senior player asked me later in the game why I sang the song. I simply answered him, "Because they deserve the national anthem."

Putting on this HAT: If you are celebrating a truly inclusive community, *all* has to mean *all*, including your special-needs population and its programming. The singing of the national anthem was more than a last-second strategy to give those student-athletes the full game experience. It was a true lesson in leadership for the members of the football team who bore witness to the event. Sometimes you have to do what you need to, despite your comfort level. School leaders must model expectations every day, especially when they can't find the music cable.

I was invited to sing at Unified Basketball's next home game. After my second—and *final* appearance—I have added *National*

Anthem Performer to my professional resume. There have been no formal inquiries since.

The Pledge: Take Two
Andrew Marotta

I love having kids say The Pledge of Allegiance. I think it shows pride for their country and school, leadership, and a sense of community. They get on the loudspeaker for all to hear. For a while, we were having the Pledge air live on the local radio station, too, which was pretty cool. During Covid, we did it live on Google Meets. Most times, it is just the old-fashioned school loudspeaker.

Often, the kids would get the giggles. They would start like you've heard a thousand times, "I pledge allegiance, to the flag . . ." Then it would hit, some giggle, some stuttering, and so on. Sometimes, they just put their hands over their mouths and could not continue, and, other times, they fumble through. I step in if this happens to try to guide them along.

Even though I speak to the kids about public speaking, speaking slowly, taking a deep breath, and so on, it happens. I even have the words written out in big, clear letters. People are shy and really feel uncomfortable with the whole thing, so I get it.

When they do stumble, I see them later in the day and ask them to come back tomorrow. Most are confused, looking at me, like "Why?"

I ask them to come back for several reasons. Life isn't about how many times we goof or screw up. It *is* about the times that we get back up, get going again, and make good on our errors. What did we learn as kids? It is not falling off the horse that matters, it is that you get back on and keep on riding. Winners have failed more often than unsuccessful people. Winners keep rolling, keep trying.

When that student or group of students come back the next day, I'll say something like, "Maria had a little case of the giggles yesterday, but she is here today to nail it."

The kid is proud afterward, and everyone who heard that student fumble the day before, also heard them get it right. It *grows* their level of respect. Teachers, staff, and others say things like, "Way to go!" because they got it right!

While many think this might be inconsequential, I believe it is a big deal. It says a lot about the person—again, not that they had a misstep, but that they righted a wrong.

Putting on this HAT: Give people that public opportunity to get it right!

The Collective Resume
Jay Billy

In our schools, so many people do so much. There is constant motion and commotion. Sometimes we fail to recognize the greatness that we have within our staff and our community. Often, we get to know a lot about people and the team we work with just by talking to them and having general conversations about them and their families. But most educators I know are very humble, so we don't always know some of their special skills or talents. In fact, staff don't always share some of their passions and special skills with their colleagues.

I believe that in order to become great as a school, we have to build toward collective efficacy—we need to know and value those we work with. Last year, I wanted to hit the re-start button on building those relationships and getting to know our staff in a different way. As we headed into our opening days of professional development and classroom preparation, I felt it was important to come back together, get to know each other, inspire one another, and really have some fun. I was looking for a good way to start this off.

One day, I was on a Twitter chat, and I saw this activity called "The Collective Resume." This was the perfect activity for our staff to get to know each other better and to really understand the amount of experience and greatness in the room.

Opening day is always one of my favorite days because it gives me the opportunity to set the tone for the year, and it's important to bring enthusiasm along with the purpose. I opened the meeting by welcoming everyone back, introducing new staff members, and sharing the agenda. We discussed the district goals and the strategic plan, all necessary things but not really exciting. Then I spoke again about collective efficacy. I use Hattie's definition from *Visible Learning*: "Collective Efficacy—A group's shared belief in its conjoint capability to organize and execute the course of action required to produce given levels of attainment." In order to move toward collective efficacy, you must believe in each other. In order to believe in each other, you must first know each other. This led us into building our collective resumes.

Since I had about 65 staff members, I had them break up into groups by grade level and specialty areas. I gave each person a sheet of paper, on which they had to answer four questions:

🎩 Years of experience in education.

🎩 Teaching certifications.

- Your strengths. Things you are knowledgeable about or showcase your talent.

- Special skills (personal or professional).

Once they'd spent about 10 minutes writing and reflecting, they spread out as a group and moved to the hallways to put their "collective" answers on a piece of poster paper. The staff spent a lot of time on this and really enjoyed learning about each other.

It really opened my eyes and the eyes of everyone else to see that we had a collective experience of more than 824 years in education. We also had some fun learning about special skills such as "dungeon master, opera singer, and chicken whisperer." Each group then walked around and looked at each poster that had been created. In the end, I took all of the posters and consolidated the information; I made a poster that is displayed in our office. I gave a copy of the poster to each staff member. We now have a reminder of the greatness that is present in our school on a daily basis as we work together in building collective efficacy.

Putting on this HAT: Activities where staff get to know each other and find out little things about one another often lead to deeper conversations. Deeper conversations help staff be vulnerable with each other, leading to building more trust. When teachers believe in one another, trust one another, and listen to one another, we can then start building the collective efficacy that is needed to become a great school. Find simple ways for staff to share their expertise and their passions. You'll find that you will quickly become a more cohesive team.

Build a Rallying Cry
Andrew Marotta

I heard once at a veteran teacher's retirement party that one thing that made this teacher so special was that he did *not* work for 30 years. He worked one year 30 different times. He made each year unique and different. Regardless of your role, I think it's important that we do this as educators: make each year special.

One way to do this is to have a rallying cry, or theme for staff, students, and parents each year. Make each year different by creating a theme based on what is happening in and around the school.

During the school year 2022–2023, we were under a major construction project in Port Jervis, New York. Our 100-year-old middle school was under construction, and we were displaced and moved to the other complex. During the hiring season, I always like to ask new hires to show their gifts and talents. During the art-teacher interviews, I asked one candidate to create a burst of *Port Pride*—make some sort of artwork that represented our school, community, and the small city of Port Jervis. She was not from the area, so I was curious to see what she would come up with.

Well, she got our attention big time. In less than two hours, she produced this image and the wording: Moving Full Steam Ahead Together.

We liked it so much that not only did we hire her as our art teacher, we made her picture and slogan our theme for the year. *Moving Full Steam Ahead Together.*

Putting on this HAT: I look back at the themes from years past and reflect. Each year, each person and each moment was unique and special in its own way. Create themes for each year that people can rally around and feel part of. Is it a special anniversary year? Is there a new wing opening? Is the community celebrating something special that the school can tie into? All ideas and thoughts about creating this heartfelt act qualify as candidates.

Here are some themes we used in the past at Port Jervis:

- 🦫 *Carry the Banner.*

- 🦫 *We're All in This Together.*

- 🦫 *This Is the Year.*

- 🦫 *Enjoy the Journey.*

- 🦫 *Cultivators of the Pride.*

- 🦫 *#GoPort!*

Mr. Joseph Case High School
Brian McCann

At a school-leadership meeting in the fall last year, the high school educator team discussed a difficult topic: shortfalls in funding. The problems were not about books, resources, or tech needs. We were discussing how smaller clubs don't generate funds but have frequent and costly bills to pay each year.

It had gone well beyond a few hundred dollars for the math team or the mock-trial dues. Each event cost money. Even more money was needed if we hosted competitions and had to feed hundreds of students, their chaperones, and the adjudicators of the meet.

We were beyond the point of more local solicitation for donations. We needed a fundraiser, one that thought outside of our box and did not involve "selling" a product. We needed something that would grab the community as well.

Area schools had been successful in a mock beauty pageant for its male students. It would involve vacation apparel, formal wear, and a "talent." We would have an opening number with all contestants.

The student-council advisor stepped up to coordinate this and received lots of help from our theater department. Senior female members of the student council decided to repurpose last year's prom gowns to give a Hollywood-style appearance to the event.

And at the end of the evening, we would crown Mr. Joseph Case High School. It's really just a fundraiser, more of a beauty pageant with a wink rather than a traditional competition. Money-raising is a serious business, but we didn't take ourselves too seriously.

The auditorium was packed this night. We were grateful to get a sponsor from a local formal-wear business that had traditionally been a great friend of the high school's theater program. The generous owner even donated a free prom tux to the winner!!

In the end, the junior-class president beat out two football captains for the first declaration of Mr. Joseph Case High School. The next year, he presented his crown to our next winner: the marching band's drum major. I'm grateful that this annual event has continued at the school after my retirement.

By the way, the math team and mock-trial participants have never had to have a bake sale since to raise money.

Putting on this HAT: Sometimes you have to embrace opportunities to laugh at yourself. The chance for a community to cheer for each other far outweighs the sexist roots of beauty pageants. Here's another example where risk-taking paid off.

CHAPTER 2

HEROES WEARING HATS

New York State Teacher of the Year
Andrew Marotta

Carolyn Dorritie is an amazing teacher and person. For years, I watched Carolyn make math fun, interesting, and relevant to kids. She teaches with enthusiasm and passion, and reaches kids by making connections and being genuine.

Anyone around Carolyn knows she's special. She is humble and would never toot her own horn. But why couldn't we?

We took action. We, teacher-leaders, administrators, students, parents, and others all got together and nominated Carolyn for the New York State Teacher of the Year. I'm not sure who was more excited—those who nominated her or Carolyn . . . it was just a great ride.

There was a lot to do: interviews, classroom recordings, visitations, essays, pictures, media, and more. It was *a lot*, but it was all worth it. Carolyn was like a proud momma through it all: hugs, smiles, and a *What else do we need to do?* attitude. She never said "no," "not now," or "I'm too busy." Like with most things with

Carolyn, she did it all with grace, strength, and pride for her family and school.

She took second place. I felt like someone took a knife and ripped open the hot-air balloon that was soaring proudly over our school community, Port Jervis, New York. How could this be? She was a star—*our* star—and they didn't choose her? With all she had done and was doing?

Putting on this HAT: After a couple of days of me moping around that we didn't win (yes, *"we,"* because we were all in on this), Carolyn warmly hugged me and said it was okay. She continued, stating that it was an honor to be nominated, and she encouraged us to look at all the positive attention it had brought to the school. Look at all the good we uncovered because we were searching for it, talking about it, and living it. Looking to highlight "the good" was in the forefront of all of our minds.

Carolyn continued to be celebrated at the school-board meetings, in her classes, and in the community. The second-place finish did not stop those who Carolyn had impacted from posting about it, letting her know, and more. All in all, it brought tremendous pride to our school and well-deserved recognition to Carolyn; it reignited our passions for nominating others for awards. Success breeds success. It was an awesome process, and I encourage you to find that special educator and nominate them for that award. Win or not, it will bring a lot of positivity to your school community. Here is one of the many articles that were written about Carolyn and this well-deserved honor: https://bit.ly/HATSTeacheroftheyear

Fast-forward this HAT: In 2018, Carolyn was accepted into the New York State master

teacher program—a program designed to train excellent teachers and make them even better. Put the really good ones around other good ones, and great things are going to happen. Guess what? It did. A second math teacher in Port Jervis Schools joined, followed by a science teacher in 2022. These teachers, along with other amazing staff with growth mindsets, are continuing to move our district forward by taking on these applications and wearing these HATS.

Make My Day
Brian McCann

Last spring, I received a phone call in my office from a fifth-grade teacher. Not *any* fifth-grade teacher.

My fifth-grade teacher.

I had been an awkward, academically minded, sort-of-shy student in her fifth-grade class in 1972.

And she called me in my office more than 50 years later.

Earlier that week, the local paper had run a very nice story about my retirement from the high school after being there for more than 35 years (including my own high school years). I had spent the past 18 years as the high school's principal.

And Mrs. Sowersby called me.

I was instantly catapulted back to my days of wearing Tuff-Skins pants, wide-collared shirts, and Converse sneakers. I was a ten-year-old once again for a few minutes. I remember her as being a risk-taker who was not afraid to do things differently, from the way she arranged her classroom, to her prioritization of relationships, to how she embraced student voice half a century before it was fashionable.

Mrs. Sowersby called to tell me two things: that she was proud of all that I had accomplished as an educator, and that she loved me.

I told her that I loved her as well and that her positive, encouraging influence on me was reflected in every interaction I had with students, any risk that I took, and any failure that I was able to learn and move forward from.

I love to hear when school leaders make positive phone calls to families, or spearhead students making good phone calls of the day. Positive affirmation continues to be validating and transformative at the same time.

But the gift of affirmation from my own teacher after that many years might have been the most valued retirement present I ever received.

Putting on this HAT: Never underestimate the power behind the human voice, even if it's been decades since you've seen a student. It is even easiest these days to send an old student a little love and recognition digitally and even through social media channels.

You're never too old to make a positive phone call.

Or receive one.

Thank you, Mrs. Sowersby, for continuing to shape me to become a better person tomorrow.

I Wish I _____ a Sister Like That
Andrew Marotta

Domonique would visit her brother Miguel each year on New Year's Day. They were close and kicked off the New Year together at brunch. They would talk about their families, goals for the year, and their lives, and reminisced about their childhood.

Domonique was the CEO of an investment company and did quite well financially. This year, she picked Miguel up in a brand-new electric car. It was like a rocket ship with all the bells and whistles. "Wow," Miguel shared when he got in and told his sister he loved it. The two had a wonderful brunch, and at the conclusion of the meal, Domonique offered for Miguel to drive. When they arrived back at Miguel's home, she wished him a Happy New Year and said, "I hope you like your new car!"

Miguel was initially confused, not understanding that his sister was gifting him the car. "OMG!" Miguel shouted with joy, thanking his sister so much for the very generous gift.

A few days later, Miguel was washing the car in his driveway, shining up his already shiny new car.

His neighbor was walking by and said, "Hi, Miguel—nice car."

Miguel proudly replied, "My sister gave it to me."

"Really," shared the neighbor, "that's incredible." Then she paused for a moment, stared at Miguel and the car, and said, "Ya know, I wish I could____a sister like that."

Putting on this HAT: What do you think the neighbor said? What would you have said? What would most people say? Think about your answer for a moment. This book is about doing for others. Giving to others in special unique ways. I wish____a sister like that.

Yes, most people will answer **had.** I wish I *had* a sister like that. It is our natural instinct to want to receive. It's OK. It's natural. It is our hope that this book will make you think, make you act in a way to serve others, and not just want to receive. Education is special. Education is memorable. Education is life-changing. I wish I could *be* a sister like that. I wish I could be an educator like that. I wish I could give of myself like that.

I love this story. It makes me think. It makes me reflect. It makes me want to do more. **Wear this HAT** to serve others, and you will never go wrong.

Lights! Cameras! Mr. T!
Brian McCann

During the 18 years I spent running the same high school, I saw the sunrise and sunset of many teaching careers. I also had the good fortune to bear witness to educators who "shifted" mid-career to try something new. This unintentional modeling of risk-taking brought new life into many careers in education and, in many cases, changed the direction of an entire school.

One such teacher was Mr. T. Mr. T came to the high school from our district's middle school, where he taught 8th-grade English for many years. When an opening availed itself in our computer department, particularly with our popular video classes, he transferred to the high school.

This career adjustment caused a brand-new dynamic at our school: a dynamic that focused on risk-taking, trust, creativity, and some old-fashioned fun.

Before Mr. T ventured into public education, he was a filmmaker and supplemented his day job with a parallel career in video production. He worked with numerous production companies and formed his own, locally, for commercial and industrial projects.

What Mr. T had was an authentic application of knowledge in video that the high school did not have previously. He not only had the tools and technique: Mr. T had the war stories of experience to validate the film theory that he was teaching his students.

One early indication that this revitalized program was on the road to success was when he asked me if he could use our flex time built into each morning (a 30-minute period that is known as "the bubble" at my school) for a silent film festival. He would use the high school's Learning Commons as a venue and open it up to any class that was interested in viewing student work.

The class's first project was the silent film, where students could focus almost solely on the visual element of film.

The weeks leading up to this event were busy at school. Small groups of students could be found in the halls, in common spaces, and in open classrooms at almost any time during the school day. Film crews might arrive early at the school for a shoot or be the last to leave the building in the afternoon.

These crews were often supervised by Mr. T, but, realistically, he could not be in multiple places concurrently. Mr. T developed *relationships* based on trust with his students. And this trust resonated whenever a shoot was conducted during the school day.

The reaction of the school was impressive as well. Because filming became commonplace, it almost transitioned as the norm of student life. And the students who were producers, directors, members of the crew, or actors were from all grades and social demographics of the high school. Take any one film, and you might see an athlete, thespian, class officer, or an NHS member working alongside another student who had not yet found a connection to the school.

The same was evident at the first showing.

I was expecting a small group of 15–20 students. What I found was the Learning Commons packed day after day with students and teachers who wanted to learn more about Mr. T's program and celebrate the initial work that had been done.

Was it fun to see students and teachers in these films? You bet! This first silent-film festival was the springboard to many future film experiences in the school, culminating each year with an Oscar-style award ceremony celebrating local filmmaking called *The Tweets*.

Putting on this HAT: The energy and passion of one person can infuse an entire school with joy. Mr. T did that for us. And his love of film and the dedication he demonstrated each day to his students became the trajectory that helped the school evolve into a model 21st-century secondary school.

Be a Mr. Jensen
Andrew Marotta

I love stories that inspire. In this impactful, true story, Clint Pulver could not sit still in class, always tapping, snapping, and moving. He couldn't sit still and kept getting in trouble. One day, Mr. Jensen called Clint over to his desk. Right away, Clint thought he was in trouble *again*. Instead, Mr. Jensen reassured Clint that he wasn't in trouble and asked him this question: "Have you ever thought about playing the drums?" He then handed young Clint a set of drumsticks and told him to have at it. Tap, hit, and strike away—and, man, did this work! He said, "Clint, you are not a problem. I think you are a drummer." Clint not only started to tap, he went on to have a highly successful career as a drummer, speaker, author, and more. Because Mr. Jensen **put on this HAT,** he changed the course of Clint's life.

Aren't these stories amazing? These HATS are examples of the power of heartfelt acts that happen all the time—simple-but-impactful, life-changing events that totally altered the lives of those on the receiving end. How can we recognize these moments when they arise? How do we know what to do? To say?

I think it imperative that we act with the mindset of "the power of a single experience." That one, simple, heartfelt act can change the course of someone's life. These can happen all day, every day in schools, and, when we believe it, we live it. When we believe it, we look to make it happen. There are countless examples throughout this book of not only nice, heartfelt acts but also life-changing acts.

It is important that we look for them, recognize these opportunities, and act on them. You never know which one will be a Mr. Jensen moment, a **Mr. Jensen HAT.**

You can hear Clint tell the story in this clip: https://bit.ly/HATSMrJensen

Putting on this HAT: I think it is so important that we keep these stories in the forefront of our minds. When dealing with kids and adults in school, especially when it is a negative situation, how can we turn it around? Shift our paradigm. In this HAT, Mr. Jensen could have easily just punished Clint over and over, but he went about it a little differently. We share another story in chapter seven, called "The Red Bicycle." In both these powerful stories, adults altered the lives of the children they were dealing with by turning a negative into a positive. When you are looking for good, alternative solutions, or just through a different lens, you can have a tremendously different outcome. Thank you, Mr. Jensen. Thank you to all the Mr. and Mrs. Jensens out there making a difference.

Who's the Boss?
Brian McCann

Who is really running your school? It goes beyond your superintendent, assistant principal, building principal, or department head. I would venture to say that the schools that operate the most efficiently are indeed effective because of the building's first line of defense: the administrative assistant, formerly known in my youth as the school secretary.

As Arthur Miller declares in his masterpiece *Death of a Salesman*, "Attention must be paid." The school's lead administrative assistant—sometimes its *only* administrative assistant—is not only the *first* voice and face that a visitor comes into contact with—for many, the admin assistant represents the face of the school.

Evelyn—not her real name—would not like any spotlight. She arrives at school almost an hour before her official start time. By the time I was in my office and teachers were starting their pre-morning rituals, Evelyn had already arranged any substitute coverage, printed schedules and class rosters, and made suggestions for any coverage switch that needed to be made.

Evelyn knew the names of all students. She knew the frequent flyers to the main office: Who needed a pencil, who needed some money for the vending machine, who might need a snack from the school nurse.

Evelyn fielded requests for early dismissals, excused absences, and athletic waivers for players who may have had a doctor's appointment on a game day. She knows who plays sports, who is in the play, and who has just come back from a family vacation.

She compiles the day's newsletter, keeping school events and sports scores up to date for public dissemination.

Evelyn edits the school's weekly informational missive to families, making suggestions for clarity and correcting typos. She keeps teachers informed about the upcoming field trips and ensures that the school has all the permissions and safety information. She double-checks the bus and will update the event's roster to reflect any student absence that day.

Evelyn knows when to call an ambulance and when to notify our local safety officials. In a crisis situation, she is in the inner circle of planning and implementation of alternate procedures.

Evelyn keeps the principal on task, reminding the leader about pending deadlines as well as providing a historical perspective of what we should be focusing on this week.

The facilitation of school administration is more than a job for Evelyn: it is a passion. She prides herself on a well-oiled machine. She takes her job both professionally and personally.

Putting on this HAT: Schools cannot be run by one person. A partnership with your administrative assistant is necessary for your building to thrive. I was blessed with many years with Evelyn. When I retired, she had to prepare the school's next leader.

There is no better mentor for a principal than the school's lead administrative assistant.

The Power of Music
Jessica Stokes

Jessica is a K-5 general music teacher, elementary choral director, and beginning band director at two elementary schools in the Delaware Valley School District in northeastern Pennsylvania. In addition to being a passionate music educator, Jessica is proud to be both a wife and the mother of two daughters. She met Andrew because she was lucky enough to be the music teacher for all three of his children!

As an educator, I teach with one goal in mind: light a spark to last a lifetime. How lucky I am, then, to be a music educator, to teach that which is all around us, all the time, in every facet of our lives! To me, music is something that unifies the world, that brings people together, and that touches our souls in an inexplicable way. "Lighting a spark" in my classroom means giving my students the tools, skills, and confidence to become lifelong participants in music, whether that be through singing, playing instruments, or simply clapping along at a concert. In the 2022–2023 school year, my classroom received a massive musical gift to further this goal: 30 beautiful ukuleles.

All of my students, from kindergarten through fifth grade, were immediately drawn to the ukuleles, and all of them have learned to play. My students feel like rock stars! Each grade level has learned something a little different, and they are completely hooked. The youngest have learned to strum and to play one or two chords, enough to sing a few age-appropriate songs. The oldest have learned to play up to five chords, have been able to sing and play along to a plethora of favorite songs, and have even learned to create their own songs to perform. My students have fallen so in love with the ukuleles that I have received countless emails from parents, requesting links to purchase ukuleles for their children so they can continue to play at home. A spark has been ignited here; my students are now seeking out further musical learning, on their own time, outside of school!

These 30 beautiful ukuleles proudly hang on a wall in my classroom, directly across from my doorway. Every person who enters my classroom, or even stops in my doorway, has a perfect view. Let me tell you: 30 ukuleles are an impressive, inviting, and downright tantalizing thing to behold. Not just for the students! After several weeks of looking at this wall of wonder, my colleagues began asking about the ukuleles. And asking again. And again. Thus, the Shohola Elementary School Staff Ukulele Club was born.

We all know that educators are busy people, constantly on the go, and consistently without enough time to do all of the many tasks already on our overflowing plates. With this in mind, while pushing my own overflowing plate to the side, I hesitantly sent the first email to my entire staff, introducing our Staff Ukulele Club in a very low-key, noncommittal manner, completely unconvinced that anyone would actually come on a Friday morning at the start of our contract hours. I planned a simple ukulele lesson: learn to strum, learn to play one chord, and learn to sing and play "Put the Lime in the Coconut." And then I waited.

There was not a single response to my email. Not one. But Friday morning came, and suddenly my room was full of nearly a dozen colleagues excited to learn something new. They were excited to pick up an instrument, to struggle, to sing, to learn, to play, to make music. Together, we found joy! My colleagues were thrilled to do something completely different and totally unrelated to their own everyday jobs. To my pleasant surprise, they keep coming back! Sometimes, we are a small handful of teachers. Often, my principal comes to join us. On our most successful club day, every single one of my 30 ukuleles was in the hands of a school professional (even our superintendent)! Some of my colleagues have even purchased their own ukuleles and practice on their own at home. I consider this to be another spark successfully lit in the music room.

Our Staff Ukulele Club has created a small shift in our building's culture. It is a moment of pure creativity, joy, magic, and collaboration. Every staff member leaves the Ukulele Club feeling uplifted and ready to face their day. There is not a lot of time dedicated to this: it is a mere 15 to 20 minutes on Friday mornings, but it has been incredibly impactful. As for me, is there really anything more I can ask for than to have my entire building believe in the power of music? I think not.

Putting on this HAT: Make this creative opportunity for your staff. What is your talent? Where do you derive joy? Perhaps it is through music: playing an instrument, singing, or even dancing. Perhaps it is through exercise or creating art or cooking. Your group may start small, but that's okay! Word will spread, joy is contagious, and your teachers will surprise you (and themselves)!

Madame
Brian McCann

Madame was my seventh-grade French teacher in the early 1970s. I had no previous experience with a different language, but her passion in the classroom captivated my adolescent attention. Her approach was hands-on and practical. We learned the vocabulary of things we came into contact with every day. Because pre-teens live in the moment, we seemed to concentrate exclusively on the present tense and trying to make sense of which nouns are masculine or feminine. We learned to conjugate verbs in French at a time we didn't even know how to formally do it in our own vernacular!

Madame was demanding and created a classroom infused with fun. She had a French name for every one of her students and learned two monikers for each of her students when some teachers couldn't remember just one.

Looking back: every time we opened our mouths and foreign sounds emanated that began to sound like words, we took a risk. Heck, Madame modeled risk-taking before it was fashionable some four decades later.

We learned a five-line dialogue that we repeated every day for the entire year:

> *J'entre dans la salle de classe.*
> *Je regarde autour de moi.*

Je vois les élèves et le professeur.
Je dis BONJOUR au professeur.
Je prends ma place.

I excelled in this class at a time when I did not have any confidence as a student. I even received a French Award at the end of the school year in our annual assembly. I had a new French teacher in eighth grade, but Madame tapped me to play the lead in a translated scene from a Molière comedy that would be performed in front of the school as part of our foreign-language week. It was my first formal experience on the stage.

Fast-forward some 15 years, and I am beginning a teaching career. Madame had transferred from middle school to high school, and it was good to reconnect in the late 1980s. We had seen each other during the summer from time to time, since we belong to the same beach club. Now we were teaching peers, though her classroom pedagogy and management system far outperformed mine.

And she was always *Madame* to me. Never by her first name. Never in English.

Later, we worked together as I became the assistant principal and subsequently the building leader. Madame retired briefly but then returned to the high school for almost 15 more years as a part-time teacher. Our French program had sunsetted, as had our Latin program. Madame taught Spanish for the last years of her teaching career.

When schools closed temporarily in March 2020, I watched Madame attack this new challenge with the same energy she's filled me with in the 1970s. She not only learned how to teach via Google Meets and deliver a curriculum exclusively through

Google Classroom, but she also availed herself via cell phone to her students seemingly around the clock.

It's possible that she connected more with her students during COVID than many teachers do face-to-face.

She still was highly organized, highly engaging, and had a Spanish name for each of her students. She did not let a pandemic stand in the way of truly teaching her students. She never complained that she had to learn new, digitally infused strategies but accepted these challenges as what good teaching looked like in 2020.

Putting on this HAT: Don't let age and experience shade an impression that the best 21st-century teaching is conducted only by those new to education. She became the model for all teachers in the building. Madame's *chapeau* combines experience, curiosity, and love for her students.

By the way, Madame came to my dad's wake when he passed. As she greeted my family in line, my sisters and I joined hands and recited with Madame:

"J'entre dans la salle de classe . . ."

Together, we recited the dialogue that we had internalized so many years ago, still reverberating our youth in our minds, and solidified for us the power behind impactful, personal relationships.

Fill the Room
Austin Wilson

Austin Wilson is an amazing educator and teacher leader from Port Jervis, New York. He teaches with passion, enthusiasm, and a love of learning and children. He gives his all in and outside the classroom. He models HATS in so many ways, and we are grateful to have him teaching in Port Jervis!

The simple act of taping a sign to a door yields much more than a smile. To me, that was my only goal: to make one of my colleagues smile by sharing a sign that recognized and celebrated her birthday. At my desk, markers glided across a poster, revealing a colorful, handwritten message in calligraphy. The sign welcomed all into the classroom and planted seeds of joy, celebration, and positivity. Seeing how this one sign was able to fill a room with love and laughter, I knew that this would be a new tradition.

For each staff member's birthday, a hand-drawn sign is hung above their classroom door. The sign reminds staff and students not only of an important date but also of the importance of being kind, of being together, and of being present. Currently, in my third year of teaching, signs have become my specialty. Signs for birthdays, baby showers, welcome-back celebrations, anything you can think of. I have been able to use my love of art to fill my cup and the cups of all those around me.

Being so young in the profession, I have seen firsthand the importance of forming a family with the people in your building. Whether it be your classroom neighbor, the custodian who cleans your room, or the cafeteria staff who feed you and the students, making each person feel genuinely appreciated and noticed is of utmost importance.

Putting on this HAT: It is quite simple to wear this type of HAT. You need to reflect and find a passion that you want to share with others. Once you decide on your "specialty," create a product, and share it with all those around you. Do it anonymously. Do it, and expect nothing in return. Do it with the purest intentions. No matter what you create, the reactions and positivity that result from sharing it will create a domino effect. One small act can change one's day and create the spark needed to change the workplace atmosphere.

Putting on this HAT for Austin: How do you repay someone's kindness? You model what you see from them: *Be Kind!* It was so heartwarming on Austin's birthday to see what happened. The staff and kids decorated his room for him. Some even tried to copy his beautiful calligraphy, writing "Happy Birthday" in French (Austin is a French teacher). This was a beautiful HAT that warmed our school that day and beyond. I thank Austin for his amazing passion for teaching and care for others. He is a true hero for many.

Saved by the Class President
Brian McCann

I was on vacation with my family when I learned about the Parkland shooting at a Florida high school. School was not in session in my town when a nationwide student walkout was being organized as a grassroots protest to stop school shootings.

When I returned to school, however, an alternate walkout day was scheduled, and students in my school became interested in being part of this second national event.

Safety was a top priority at my school, one that I share with schools across this country and the world. Single entrances during the school day were the norm. Security cameras increased each year. Established and practiced protocols were in place for any number of emergency situations.

After conferring with the central office and making sure we were in accord, I gathered the elected student leaders from each class to acknowledge what they were feeling, give power to their voices, and present what some of the limitations would be in an organized student walkout.

First and foremost, no one could physically leave the building. We would give them a safe space with sound equipment, so that students would have an appropriate venue within the confines of our student handbook.

Because of how we are situated, there was no safe outside venue for an impromptu protest. We decided that the auditorium would be the safest and most secure venue.

We met again to answer questions from the student leadership and penciled in a time when the walkout would occur.

There would be no bell, no announcement, no summons to the event.

With the exception of two students, no one left the building. Students met for about 30 minutes, voiced their concerns, called for action, and returned to class.

And then social media erupted. Someone told a parent that doors were being barred, students were being held in the gym against their will, and their voices were being squelched. Other people from outside the town took these inaccuracies and started to make terrible accusations against the school administration—most specifically, *me*.

The media picked up on this and wanted a response.

The senior class president saved the day. Ava had been part of the planning from the beginning of the week and could attest to the careful and mindful plans that went into making this a safe event for students.

Most importantly, she had the courage to set the record straight on social media, which began a string of defenses from other students that the situation had been handled correctly in school.

Ava went on record with the local paper in defense of her school and her principal and literally stopped the social-media bleeding that had erupted.

President Ava saved the day for me. As much as the reporter wanted to believe my perspective, the details of the day—from planning to fruition—were validated by an 18-year-old student leader.

Putting on this HAT: When you partner with students, you are more likely to have a positive outcome. Did it help that I already had a strong relationship with the class president? That I spoke with her almost every day of the school year? That I had included her in other school-based decisions?

Once again, the power of relationships and how they build integrity in your building cannot be underestimated. Relationships may not only save the day but also help promote a positive school-leadership image beyond your local community.

CHAPTER 3

INTENTIONAL HATS

Shadow a Student
Andrew Marotta

Blocking out a whole day and shadowing a student for the duration of their schedule seems like a daunting task. *I have so much to do. I'm so busy. There is no way I can do that. I just can't afford that time.*

I've said all these and heard all of these, but this act is so worth it. It helped me build relationships with my students, shifted my lens on how I viewed things in my school, and helped me walk in their shoes. It also gave me a deeper look at the staff. I got to see and experience teachers for their whole lesson and not just a glimpse or a piece.

Two experiences that really stick out to me are these: First: time. For years, I coached teachers to get started immediately with their lessons. A do-now, an opening ticket, a quick assessment. Something to get the students engaged immediately. Well, by period 3, my head was spinning. Start this, open this, read this, finish this, write this . . . It was all so much too quick. I had no time to digest it and process it. I just had to do it . . . eight times that day. After reflecting on this experience of shadowing a student for the day, I see the need for a few minutes to sit and breathe. This gives the students a moment to think about what they are going to start doing, which was totally different from just starting it right away after coming in from the busy, hectic hallways.

The second point I really took away was #FrontRow. I shadowed a freshman and a senior this one particular year, and the senior sat in the front row of every one of his classes. I noticed this during period three, and we had a discussion about it. He shared, "You *get more* up front" and "There are fewer distractions . . . It is just the teacher and the learning in front of you." I was extremely impressed and offered this advice to many students afterward.

Putting on this HAT: Make the important thing the important thing. This day (shadowing a student for the day) is so meaningful. You can learn so much about your school, your staff, your students, and more. Schedule it. Bring an open mind, an open book, and absorb it all.

Principal for the Day
Jay Billy

Embracing similar tenets of Andrew's student-based focus, a principal shadow day can also be a valuable experience.

Our school PTO does many amazing events and activities for our students and their families. Some of the best things that happen at our school occur because the PTO sponsors them or has an idea. These special events all cost money to put on, and our PTO has a variety of ways to raise money. We try to have a good mix of free events, where all kids can participate, and events where families will be charged for participation. One thing we always make sure is that any student who wants to participate can participate, no matter the cost. We find ways to involve every student. Whether it be through donations, dine-to-donate participation, the Scholastic Book Fair, or special events where money is charged for participation, the money raised is used for all students.

One of the fundraisers that our PTO has done for years is called a Teacher Time Auction. Teachers volunteer their time for special events and activities for a small number of students. Parents and kids purchase a roll of raffle tickets and put them in bags associated with special activities. This is a very popular fundraiser for our families. Again, our PTO is mindful of certain families who may not be able to financially participate, so they find ways to make sure students who want to be part of this, can be.

Some examples of these Teacher activities are:

- Cupcake making with Mrs. Carnevale

- Drawing class with Mrs. Skorupa

- Pizza lunch with Mrs. Smoots

- Lunch and Story Time with Mr. Brackett

Then students buy raffle tickets with their names and numbers on them, and put them into a basket/bag, and hope they get picked.

Over the years, I've offered up things like, "Snow Day Read Aloud at Your House," "Lunch with the Principal," or "Driveway

Shoveling by the Principal." One of the most popular Principal Time Raffles has been the "Principal for the Day." Each year, this is one of the fullest baskets we have, and our PTO always makes it the last basket drawn so that students wait around to see who the winner will be.

When a student wins "Principal for the Day," I try to make it amazing for them. I first talk to the student's teacher to pick a day when there will be very little educational-impact loss. Once we've established a day, I make sure that my schedule is clear, and then I build a schedule for the "Principal." I reach out to all of the people who work in the central office (Superintendent, Assistant Superintendent, Director of DEI, Director of Personnel, Director of Special Services, and our Curriculum Supervisors). I schedule meetings for the "Principal" with each of them during their day. Once these are established, I make a schedule for the day.

Here is a copy of one schedule:

8:00–8:10	Meeting/Assign Subs
8:10–8:40	Bus Duty
8:40–8:50	Supervise Clap-In
8:50–9:30	Check-in Classes
9:30–9:50	Meet with Curriculum Supervisors
9:50–10:10	Meet with Director of Personnel, Asst. Superintendent
10:10–10:30	Meet with Director of Student Services
10:35	Fire Drill
10:45	Observe Classroom Teacher
11:15	Visit classrooms
11:45	Lunch/Recess with Friends
12:30	Write Notes to Teachers

1:15–1:35	Meet with Superintendent
1:45–2:10	Check the Building
2:10–2:40	Visit Classroom
2:40–3:10	Write about Your Day
3:10–3:30	Bus Dismissal

Other things throughout the day:

- Walk the grounds and check for safety issues

- Handle discipline issues

- Play with kids during recess

- Wear funny hats and act silly

- Take pictures of the amazing things happening at school and tweet

Prior to the day, I make sure to make an official-looking badge for the "Principal" to wear. I'll put one of our "substitute" badges in the lanyard so that the "Principal" can access the doors. I'll send out a sign-up for meetings to make the schedule clear. One other thing I do that I feel is really important is send a copy of the tentative schedule home prior to the day, so that the parent can go over the schedule with the "Principal." This raises the level of excitement and generates some thought prior to this taking place.

You'll notice that I include time to visit classrooms and even observe a teacher. I always try to give feedback when I'm visiting classrooms, so I make sure the "Principal" writes notes to the teachers giving them some feedback. I also build in time for the "Principal" to be a kid, so they get to have lunch and go to recess with their friends (either in the office or the cafeteria,) depending on their preference. When meeting with the Central Office Administrators or other supervisory personnel, I'll give the "Principal" some simple questions to ask. This is a great opportunity for the Central Office People to get to know a little about one of our students and to also hear the student's (Principal) feelings about the school and the staff.

Putting on this HAT: This is one of the hardest days for me, as a principal. I basically have to block out the day and not do my job. I have to give this entire day to the "Student-Principal" in order to make sure that I'm giving them the best possible experience.

In the book *Teach Like a Pirate*, by Dave Burgess, he talks about creating LCLs (Life-Changing Lessons.) For these one or two kids who get the opportunity to be "Principal for the Day" each year, I believe we have created that memory of a lifetime. It's worth it, and I recommend it to all school leaders, no matter the level you work at.

The Shadow Knows
Brian McCann

Seeing a journey from multiple perspectives can be a shadow focus. What if the shadowed student then becomes the principal for a day? What happens when this continues over a high-school experience?

Caleb G. reinforced to me what it is to be a risk-taker.

I was at a community event a few years back, and a former student, who was now a school leader in another town, introduced me to a couple who had a son who was a freshman at my school. Although I knew the name from a summer of schedule finessing, I couldn't picture him. I excused myself, used my iPhone to call up the school's administrative software, and found his picture.

I took a photo with the couple and made a plan to call their son down to the office on Monday morning to share with him my newest friends.

What I didn't realize at this time was that this meeting would be the beginning of a four-year relationship.

Caleb and I connected that next Monday and developed a positive relationship during his freshman year. I would say "Hello" to the young man by name and engage him in occasional conversation. It wasn't until really the start of the school year's third term that I got the idea to partner with him in an annual event.

I had been doing annual student shadows for three years at that point, having shadowed a senior, a junior, and a sophomore in the past. I was looking at spending the day with a freshman that particular year but hadn't given any real thought to a specific student.

When I bumped into Caleb's dad at a freshman basketball game, my plan was ignited. And now, before I asked the student, I had the blessing of the parent to spend the day with his son at school. Caleb's dad also told me that it would be great if he could spend the day shadowing the principal as well.

Hmmm. A seed had been planted.

Caleb was supportive of my idea, so we chose a late-winter school day, where I would meet Caleb at his bus stop and literally spend the entire school day with him, including his bus rides. Like other shadowing experiences I had been a part of, this year was another eye-opener to what an actual school day feels like.

Since teachers know only that I will be part of a shadow experience during a specific week (rather than the specific student and teachers), an authentic school day is highly probable rather than a dog-and-pony event. I enjoyed all of Caleb's classes, the high levels of teacher engagement with students, the multiple connections children have with adults during the day, and the many critical skills and higher-order thinking opportunities that children have.

I also experienced how jam-packed the day was, with little-to-no respite for freshmen during the school day.

Later that spring, Caleb spent the day with me. And the local newspapers celebrated these experiences with front-page stories.

Caleb's school-administrator experiences were varied: from an inspection of the new track, to a scheduled teacher evaluation, to a virtual job interview, to hosting the annual administrative assistants' luncheon, Caleb told me that he couldn't believe how many times during the day that someone wanted to speak with me and the scope of information I needed to know and effectively communicate.

The mutual shadowing days were beneficial for us both. The pandemic school year thwarted a student shadow the next year, but Caleb and I agreed to do it when we returned to school for his junior year, albeit, this time, masked. I experienced firsthand how isolating this school year was for students, especially given the draconian (yet necessary) seating protocols for the entire school year.

We did receive great news coverage on our shadowing reunion.

Finally, in Caleb's senior year, we had our final shadow experience, culminating his high school journey in his final month of high school.

Because Caleb took this risk as a freshman, I was able to connect with the young man on a deeper level than with many students. I recommended him for his first job at a local sandwich shop and wrote one of his college recommendations. In return, he became one of my authentic references in my CV. Finally, Caleb was the recipient of a scholarship in my dad's name that he would use to help finance part of his first post-secondary year after high school.

Putting on this HAT: Who are your students who will help push you to a new level? Search for the young leaders in your building who will venture outside of their comfort zone to share with their administrators their school experience. There is nothing more authentic than a random and organic day in the life of a student. Risk-taking such as shadowing can have positive reverberations for years after the initial leap has been made.

Handwritten Cards
Christopher Turnbull

Christopher Turnbull is the principal at Bear Tavern Elementary School in Hopewell Township, New Jersey. Chris was named the 2022 Visionary Principal for the State of New Jersey and is in his Doctoral program at Rider University.

While I am 100 percent certain that there is no one reading this who has *not* written a card, this is one of the most effective tools in my toolbox. It goes without saying that writing a card is a motivating and kind thing to do for a staff member, but I am always surprised to see how many staff members have their old cards hanging on a bulletin board by their desks or kept in a special place.

I made a template in Microsoft Publisher many years ago with our school's logo and my name. There are two to a sheet, and I print a new batch each August (and then reprint as needed). There is no better way to highlight and reinforce a practice or a character trait or just to give a pick-me-up when needed.

So much of school, and especially classroom visits, is clouded with "accountability," "data," and "growth plans," etc. We have so many formal observations and requirements. By remembering to write a short card, we can reinforce the great stuff that we see, without having to provide something to "work on," at least in that moment, and we can build confidence, show gratitude, and create connections, all in one or two minutes.

It is such a simple task, but in the craziness of each day, it's easy to bump it down the list if we are not conscious and purposeful about sharing these small moments. Writing personalized cards is a tangible and manageable way to say, "I see you," and "Thank you," while highlighting what a staff member does well.

Putting on this HAT: First, print a bunch of cards on thick paper. Below is an example of my template. Once you print, just cut them in half and carry them around with you. I recommend keeping a list of everyone you've written a card to (or using a staff list with checkmarks), just to ensure that you are spreading positivity. It is also very helpful to schedule chunks of time (as little

as 15–20 minutes or as much as an hour) to pop around to a few classrooms with the express intent of leaving cards.

The Power of the Handwritten Note
Andrew Marotta

Winning 1st place in the Odyssey of the Mind, a broken bone, marriages, births, birthdays, winning the spelling bee, student-of-the-month recognition, losing the election: These are just a few examples of opportunities to send a handwritten note home to a student or a staff member. There are so many things happening throughout the day, yet breaking for one or two minutes to send home a personalized, handwritten note is so powerful and so impactful. Think about those old Visa commercials with the slogan, "Priceless." This is just about the same.

For fifty cents (or whatever the price of a stamp is these days), you could have a profound impact on someone in your school community. Get some super-cool, sharp school stationery or cards with your school logo and slogan on them, and start writing. Here are a few strategies I use to help manage my time and workflow regarding cards:

- Ask an office clerical staffer to help you manage these efforts.

- Gather all staff birthdays, and have that person address all the cards in chronological order.

- Look for the occasions, good and bad, positive and challenging situations.

- Get the cards written early and often.

I've written so many cards that I'd forget I'd written them. People stop and thank me for acknowledging the loss in their life, or a congratulations letter, and I'm reminded about the power of the card . . . the handwritten, personalized card. Don't use a form letter or typed note. Write the notes. You'll be pleased with the results.

Putting on this HAT: Some of the strategies in this book are deeper, more complex social situations or acts. This is *not*. This is just a simple card or letter. Just that. Yet the impact is where the HAT lies. Receiving a card in good times *and* bad is what people really appreciate—adults *and* kids. Especially the kids, though. A kid has an amazing performance at the musical? Take a moment to acknowledge this via that note and maybe, just maybe, the kid will be inspired to chase his/her dream to Broadway. A kid loses an election? Encourage them to continue their journey. Share with that student how someone lost almost 10 elections before becoming President.

Have the letters/cards at the ready, and get them in the mail. Impactful and heartfelt acts are waiting to be opened!

Staff Pajama Day
Jay Billy

The school year is 180-plus days long and sometimes can become very stressful. As a school leader, it is important to be able to under-stand the climate you are creating while still having a feel for what is going on in our buildings. There are times throughout the year that one can walk through the building and feel the stress that the staff is feeling. It's during these times that we have to help our staff and students find ways to relax. I believe that it is important that our students know that we love our jobs and that coming to school can be fun. When we become anxious and uptight, we can't be at our best.

One day last year, I was walking through the building, and I could just feel that people were feeling overwhelmed with expectations and that everyone was a bit tight. I'm not sure what it was, but everyone was on edge. I began to think of ways that I could loosen everyone up, and I came up with an idea.

Kids in elementary school love it when their teacher calls for a "pajama day." They look forward to coming to school in a relaxed way. Teachers often use "pajama day" as a reward for the work that the students have done. So . . . This is what we did. I sent an email before the end of the day telling the staff, "Tomorrow is a pajama day for staff. Don't tell the kids—just come to work in your pajamas or any comfortable clothing that you would wear around the house." I wasn't sure who would take me up on the plan, but I figured I'd try it.

The next day came, and, as staff walked through the office in the morning, many were wearing pajamas of some kind—some for comfort, some for laughs. It was evident from the beginning that the tension that I felt the day before had dissipated and that people were more relaxed. The best part was that, when the students arrived, they all thought they had missed the message. As students entered the building, they kept asking why we were all wearing pajamas. But really, this pajama day wasn't for the students—it was for the staff. The teachers had fun with it and took it on as a challenge. Whatever was causing our stress seemed to have left us. People seemed more ready to do the difficult work of being educators, and the students got to see that school can be a fun place for teachers.

Putting on this HAT: Sometimes there are reasons for tension in the building, and sometimes it just comes from a long year or month without many breaks. When you walk around your building, you can feel how everyone is feeling. When you feel that people are uptight or overly stressed, it is your job to help them. Find ways to celebrate the good we do, and make school a fun place to be. Give teachers and staff the ability to take a breath and relax. In the long run, it will make us all better and will help everyone to refill their buckets.

The Quiet Zone
Brian McCann

I remember when I first began to read education books. For whatever reason, I avoided this genre in my first few years as a school administrator—it seemed it was all I could do to keep my head above water each day. Couple this with raising three small children as my wife traveled a lot for business, and it was a wonder I did any reading at all.

But I was always a listener, and I would hear fellow principals talk about the books that they were reading. It wasn't until my first national conference that I became intentional in broadening my reading horizons to include educational philosophy, guidelines for improved leadership, and war stories from the school building into my reading lexicon.

One of the terms that entered into my world was the notion of a "hack." I came to learn that had nothing to do with gaining illegal computer access or chopping up something into pieces. A hack was a creative, original way of doing something different.

Some could result from shifting a perspective; others took some money to implement.

One of my favorite hacks early on was the transformation of an underused space in a school that was intended just for teachers. This idea came before the widespread notions of self-care and SEL for educators. Dubbed "a quiet zone," this space was comfortable, quiet, free of distraction, and lit with low-wattage lighting.

I had an office on my building's second floor that was not being used. I was able to purchase some plush, comfortable furniture through a donation from a local furniture chain and even had a few extra dollars for a new rug and some lamps. Please note: every piece of furniture came from a clearance room that had been marked down multiple times. My wife and I had to make multiple trips in our minivan to get these new items to the school, but it was well worth a few hours outside of the school day.

The notion behind this quiet zone was for teachers to be able to find a few minutes during the school day to recalibrate without fear of the unexpected question or demand "... *if they have a minute.*" The quiet zone is a highly personal space that allows therapeutic silence to weave its magic during the course of a school day, providing us with the strength necessary to resume our mission during the regular course of the day.

I introduced this new room to small faculty groups and at large staff gatherings. I encouraged people to take advantage of this social-emotional well-being opportunity whenever they wanted to during the day.

Although initially a little leery of the idea, professionals in my building started to use the space at their own pace. It was my job to remind them of this possibility in an ongoing manner.

Putting on this HAT: With a little outside inspiration, building leaders can be at the forefront of the care of your staff. Small gestures like the creation of a safe space for adults go a long way in helping to promote and sustain a positive school culture.

Ironically, I met the author who first planted this idea in my head a year later at another national conference. I thanked the author for this idea and told him about its success in my building. He asked me to forward some photos of the space to him—he hadn't known of a school up to this point that had actually brought his idea into fruition since he'd published it.

Hopefully, now, there are many zones of quiet for teachers in school buildings.

Clear Is Kind
Jay Billy

"Clear is kind. Unclear is unkind."

I attribute this to Brené Brown, who says she first heard it at an Alcoholics Anonymous meeting. To me, it just makes a lot of sense. When we avoid clarity or avoid saying what we really mean, we are not giving those we work with a clear understanding of our expectations and needs. How can anyone know the expectations of an organization if the leader of that organization is not clear about what they want?

In the spring of 2018, I was told that I was being transferred to a different school within my district. I would begin my new job on July 1 of that year. I came with the understanding that I was the third principal they had had over the past five years. Although I didn't ask for the transfer, I knew why the superintendent made the decision. In a lot of ways, it made sense. We had made great progress and growth where I was, and the school was in a good place. My superintendent told me that I was needed in this different school. Since I have worked in this district for many years, I knew what had been going on, and I knew many of the staff at the school. I had also seen and heard a lot of negative comments and information about what had been happening. I had read posts from parents on Facebook bad-mouthing the school, the principal, and the staff. I heard the rumblings from the staff about their unhappiness and loss of passion. I knew that it was going to be hard to come into a school and make changes right away, but I also knew that *some* changes had to happen immediately in order for us to move forward.

My first meeting with the families was the day before the school year ended, and I was about to take over for the next year. The PTO was doing an evening event, and they made it into a meet-and-greet. I was excited to get started but still reeling a little from leaving a school that I had grown to love. When I arrived at the event, everyone was so nice and welcoming. The kids were playing on the playground, and people came up to shake my hand and thank me for attending. At some point in the evening, I went inside the all-purpose room for a formal introduction and welcome, with about 200 parents in the room. I was asked to share some words.

I began by thanking everyone for being so welcoming and for having the event. Then I got real with everyone. I stood up with the microphone and asked, "Let me ask: What have you heard about me?" A few hands went up, and people said some nice things. As I said, I had worked in the district for 11 years, and I had been around for quite some time. It was nice to hear that people knew about me and my work. I shared a few things about myself and my family, and then I said, "Now, let me tell you what I've heard about you." At this point, I shared a few of the things I'd read on Facebook, without sharing names. These were unkind posts that were extremely critical of the school and administration. I explained to everyone, "We cannot be great if we don't begin to talk about ourselves as great. I know there are things that we need to work on and get better at, but we need to talk about them and begin the work. Posting negativity on social media doesn't help us get better and doesn't make the school that your children go to get better. We need to talk about these things and get better." I also emphasized the importance of modeling how social media can be used for good, not bad.

The crowd got very quiet. I explained further, "So if there are things that are bothering you, don't put them on Facebook. Give me a call, and we'll talk. My goal for this school is to make it the best elementary school in the state of New Jersey, and I need your help." Although I didn't speak for very long, I'm pretty sure some of the parents were very happy to hear this from me, while others were like, "Uh-oh, he's calling us out."

Throughout the summer, I didn't see much on social media that was negative about the school, but when I did, I would call the parent and have a discussion. The thing is, when you call a parent about something they put on social media, they often feel somewhat embarrassed or realize that they could have handled it differently. They also talk to their friends, who then begin to think before posting any negativity.

Once, I got a call from the superintendent's office saying a parent called because there were bees on the playground. Not a big deal, but not something the superintendent should have to deal with nor should even be contacted about. As soon as I heard, I called the parent and told the husband, "I got a call from the superintendent's office that your wife called about the bees on the playground. I wish she had called me. I'm here every day, and it's really not something the superintendent needs to be bothered with. I have already contacted an extermination company, and they were out yesterday."

The response from the husband was, "My wife did what? I'll have her call you." That afternoon, the wife did show up at my office with apologies and gifts. We also had a really good conversation and connected so that she became an advocate for our school. The word got out. I will call you to talk if I see something or hear something. *We can't be great unless we talk about ourselves as great.* It doesn't help to talk badly about our schools unless we want to fix the problems. I made it very clear that I want to fix things and be clear on the goals we set.

Putting on this HAT: Be clear in your hopes and dreams for your school. Communicate what you want and how you want things handled. Don't let others tell the story of your school without your input. Clear is kind, and people don't get to publicly call you out without having a discussion. We need to model what we hope for our students and society and clearly delineate what is expected by all who we encounter.

Schedule Emails
Andrew Marotta

The "Schedule Send" feature on email is a game-changer. I am an early riser, usually 5 a.m. on most days. I can super-focus on items without interruption and hack away at my to-do, to-accomplish list. Most of this deep work time is outside teachers' and staff's contractual workday. I have learned over time that, even though I may be working outside normal work hours, not everyone else is, nor do they appreciate receiving work information when they are not working. Sending people work items can produce the following:

- **Anxiety:** Colleagues may feel the need to complete whatever it is you sent when you send it vs. when they get back to work. It may cause unnecessary anxiety in others.

- **Pressure:** Time pressures to perform when they are not on duty.

- **Intrusive:** Even though people can choose when they look at emails, some people have notifications turned on regardless of the time. Ping! Sending that email at 8 p.m. on a Friday night while a staff member is watching a movie with their family. They quickly pop up, check the email, and start thinking about what you wrote about instead of enjoying the time with their family.

Now, the iPhone has even added the "Schedule Text" feature; you can hold the button down to schedule a text. How thoughtful and helpful to you and your colleagues.

Putting on this HAT: This is a true win-win situation. Schedule your emails and texts when working at hours outside of the normal workday. It allows you to complete the action when you are doing it, yet send it to your colleagues while they're working—not during their off-time. This shows respect toward staff and students regarding their workday; they will appreciate your protecting their so-important family time and downtime. #Scheduleit

Tag!

Jay Billy

A couple of years ago, I had the chance to hear inspirational speaker Kevin Carroll. Kevin is the author of *Rules of the Red Rubber Ball* and other books. Kevin writes and speaks about play and sports as a blueprint for life. During his session, he shared a Nike commercial (view here: https:// bit.ly/HATSTag) of a game of TAG in the city. He also talked about hundreds of employees on the grounds at Google, playing TAG. As I  watched and listened, I tried to think of how I could bring this type of fun and joy to my staff.

I came back from the conference and thought it over. I told people about the video and shared how I wanted to bring this type of fun to our school and staff. Finally, one day, it came to me. I sent out an email first thing in the morning explaining the game:

- 🎩 We are going to play TAG today, and the game will begin at 10 a.m. I am IT!

- 🎩 The person who is IT will wear a clothespin that says "IT!"

- 🎩 We will play from 10 a.m. to dismissal, when all buses have left. If you are IT at that time, you lose.

🦇 The main rule is, while playing all day, you must do your job. Teach your classes, attend to your assignments, and be where you are supposed to be throughout the day.

🦇 No re-tags (you can't tag the person who just tagged you).

🦇 At 3:20, if you are IT, report to the office.

One thing that I am proud of is that I try to get into classrooms all day long. This day's experience visiting classrooms was different. As I walked into classrooms, teachers would purposefully move to the other side of the room or circle away, not knowing if I was IT or not. I'd see classes walking down the hallway and teachers avoiding each other, not knowing if they would be tagged IT the very next minute. The students started seeing what was going on, and all laughed and giggled, seeing their teachers playing and having fun. The kids started asking me, "Are you IT?" When teachers walked into each other's classrooms, you'd see them look at each other and try to determine if it was just a regular visit or if the game was on. In some classrooms, the students would surround the teacher, protecting them from getting tagged, not even knowing if the person in the room was IT.

At the end of the day, everyone has a duty, and many are involved in helping students get on the buses or get to their cars. It's almost impossible to avoid being around other adults. Watching how everyone interacted and avoided each other was so much fun. Teachers would drop their students off at the bus and run to the parking lot to get away from everyone, knowing they didn't want to be IT at the end. I didn't tell them that the person who ended the day as IT would receive a Starbucks gift card.

Putting on this HAT: Who doesn't like to laugh and have fun? When you love your job and the people you work with, you want to make the day fun and enjoyable for everyone. Find ways to make the hard days easier and to build the community and connections of everyone you work with. When students see the staff having fun throughout the day, they will come with a different attitude, and that positivity will permeate all that you do.

Small Gifts, Big Impact
Meghan Redmond

Meghan is the 2019 NASSP National Assistant Principal of the Year as well as Alaska's 2019 Assistant Principal of the Year. She spent 11 years as a teacher and assistant principal in Bush Alaska, at Twin Hills School and Chief Ivan Blunka School, and is currently principal at Homer Middle School in Homer, Alaska.

For 11 years of my life, I lived off the road system in Bush Alaska. If you don't know what "off the road system" means, you are really missing out. It means a place that is not connected to any other communities by roads. For me, it meant my family and I had to get on a tiny airplane in Anchorage and fly to get to where we lived, landing on a gravel airstrip in the middle of the tundra. It meant everything we needed to live and to run a school—from breakfast cereal to textbooks—was flown in on small airplanes. It meant loading up our basketball team on one of those small planes to fly to a neighboring village every time they played a game. It meant if you wanted to eat a fancy breakfast or drink a caramel latte, you made it yourself. And it meant finding your people and taking care of them.

While it was an absolute blessing to experience living in one of the most amazing places on the planet, you start to miss a lot of comforts when you live in a place like that. So when you have to make a trip to Anchorage for a doctor's visit or a conference, you treat yourself. Every time my principal and best friend, Robin Jones, would fly to Anchorage, she would treat not only herself, but she would also treat our entire staff. It became a tradition for her to bring back Krispy Kreme donuts for the whole staff to enjoy upon her return.

To thank her for always spoiling us when she went to "The Big City" and being the best principal and friend I could ever ask for, I decided to pull off an epic Principal Appreciation Month surprise to show her the appreciation she deserved. I ordered 18 dozen Krispy Kreme donuts, enough for every single student and staff in the school to have one, with a whole dozen just for Robin to enjoy for herself. And of course, the tables full of donuts she was surprised with were decorated with puns like "You are an a'glaze'ing principal!"; "You are the sprinkles on the top of our school!"; and "You 'donut' know how much we appreciate you!"

Now surprising someone with 18 dozen donuts is no small feat even when you live on the road system (that's what everywhere else in the world is called when you live in Bush Alaska). But I couldn't just drive down the block to Krispy Kreme to pick them up. Weeks ahead of time, I had to order the donuts, set up for an expeditor to deliver them to an air taxi in Anchorage, have them flown out to us, pick them up from the airport, and transport them to the school on a 4-wheeler. Of course, I also had to account for inclement-weather delays and possible smushed pastries, all the while keeping the logistics and coordination efforts top secret from my best friend, whom I talked to every single day. The stars aligned, and the weather cooperated, and with a ton of help, the surprise was a huge, delicious hit!

Putting on this HAT: Everything I know about being a great principal, I learned from Robin Jones. This story shows two of those things that I use every day as a principal. Number one: *Take care of your staff—always.* Number two: *Celebrate the amazing people around you.*

When you live in Bush Alaska, you have to find your people and take care of each other. People will always do more than what is expected when they feel appreciated and know you care about them. Most of all, focusing your energy and resources on how you "treat" the people who make up your school community will ultimately create an environment where students and staff *want* to be. You will have a place where students (and staff) are happy to come to every morning and don't want to leave at the end of every day.

Mask Optional
Brian McCann

The 2021–2022 school year continued to bring uncertainty. Students, teachers, and families yearned for increasing levels of normalcy. Schools returned fully populated, no longer regulated by a cohort model. Mandatory, assigned seating in classrooms and the cafeteria went by the wayside. Athletics continued in traditional seasons, albeit now masked.

Everything seemed to focus on the mask. The battle was constant in enforcing masks to be worn properly. How many times can you say "Mask up!" during the course of a day? Unfortunately, masks seemed to be the focal point of the school day. One upside:

The school day now had built-in mask breaks as well as increased freedom for teachers to bring classes outside.

Students complained. Teachers complained. Families complained. Yet, we had great hope that things *could* change during this school year. We were bolstered by the memory that, a little less than a year before, the state reconsidered the requirement of masks when they were worn outside.

We waited patiently as the school year continued, with the hope of spring right around the corner. We looked for data that reflected decreased COVID numbers and increased vaccinations to help state authorities at least to remove the *Mandatory* moniker from mask-wearing.

The good news came right before our winter break in February—the state would ease the mandatory wearing of masks when we returned to the building on Monday, February 28.

A local radio station interviewed me and recounted the timeline on the video.

"When the state officials announced (that) we were going to go 'mask-optional,' I thought this might be a good opportunity to collaborate," McCann said.

With the help of the media and drama departments, McCann and a few of his students wrote and performed a parody music video to the iconic song "Tomorrow" from the stage musical Annie. *"We met on Monday, recorded audio on Tuesday, and filmed it on Wednesday," said McCann. "We posted it (Sunday morning) and it's fun to see people liking it."*

Here's a link to the video that went viral that day:

https://bit.ly/HATSMasksoptional

As principal, I spent almost my entire day fielding television media requests for interviews. Although some stations chose to meet virtually, we hosted live trucks from both the Providence and Boston markets.

Once again, the media is yearning for positive education stories, especially those with a hook to a local or national trend or school issue. And it all started five years ago with a snow day. More on this in Chapter 9.

Putting on this HAT: As the radio station reported, projects like this are fun and encourage a positive school culture. It also reflects leading by example. When the building leader is not afraid to take risks, it encourages all stakeholders in the school community to take chances. The modeling of the HAT of vulnerability is crucial to a healthy school.

Many thanks to FUN107 for capturing this pictorial moment from the video and curating the video's release on their website:

https://bit.ly/HATSFun107

CHAPTER 4

HATS FOR ALL SIZES

Levi's Voice
Brian McCann

As a building leader, one of my annual projects was to update plans and requests for capital improvements to the building and the campus. We have redone the gym, library, and auditorium; we have upgraded technology; we've repurposed underused spaces with programs that look like the 21st century. We've made changes for academic reasons, for access reasons, and for safety reasons.

Not every request is granted; some are penciled in for the next year; others seem to be annually bumped from the list.

Despite some upgrades to the asphalt track in the early 2000s, the space had deteriorated to the point that no home track meets could be held. The school department put together a proposal from the town to be voted on at a special town meeting for almost $300K to replace the asphalt track with a state-of-the-art rubber surface.

The new track was one of 13 articles that the town wanted to be considered. Nine of these had a price tag attached.

There's nothing unusual about the aforementioned. In our local government structure, requests occur from time to time to spend certified free cash.

Not all requests pass.

The track request had some public input. Testimony from a former track coach and high-school principal helped the voters understand *why* it was a good investment and the wide swath of student-athletes that track attracts.

Again, there is nothing unusual for advocates within the town to provide testimony.

What was unusual was the appearance of an 18-year-old senior, Levi, who had excelled at track during his high-school tenure. He was looking at post-secondary opportunities at this time so that he could continue this passion.

Levi's presence gave this proposal a face. He spoke about how schools in his athletic conference do not want their athletes coming to Case to run for safety reasons. He added the fact that the school could not host a conference meet for the past three years.

He also added that this upgrade would not affect him personally since any repair would happen after he graduated.

Putting on this HAT: Sometimes a larger issue is more palatable when you see the effect on one person. Levi took a risk by advocating for this change in a public forum. There was no safety net or pause button that evening. Levi presented the town with facts, hoping for positive change for future runners. It would create a sense of pride not only for student-athletes but for the town as a whole.

Levi's plea passed. When the track was officially opened during the next school year, Levi was invited to the opening as the school's guest of honor.

Levi indeed helped his school get back on track.

Connection: Snow Day Read-Alouds
Jay Billy

I try to show students and staff that I'm a reader and a learner by sharing books and articles I read and taking time to read stories to students. Reading is a big connector for many of our students, and, when we share stories or books, we help to build bonds through common interests. Whenever I get the chance to substitute in classrooms, my favorite part of the day is the read-aloud. Often, I'll add that to whatever the teacher has planned if it's not already part of the day's schedule. I have a large library of children's books in my office that I like to pull from, whenever I get the chance. Many times, I'll pick books that have specific themes or meanings, based on the time of the year, but other times, I choose randomly, based on something that I'm thinking about at the time.

Years ago (before Zoom, YouTube, and Google Meet), we were in the middle of winter when we had a multi-day snowstorm. Schools were closed for three days in a row after a long weekend, and I sincerely missed my connection to the kids. My energy is really connected to having students all around me, and I needed a fix. This is when I came up with an idea . . . What if I found a way to get connected to our students and share a few books? So, I researched some video platforms and figured out a way to go live on the internet. From here, I sent out an email to our families explaining that I really missed the kids and was going to do a live read-aloud on the computer, for those who wanted to join me. I asked them to join me at this certain time, and we'd have some fun.

This was the beginning of our Snow Day Read-Alouds. From here, whenever it snows, I'm able to connect with our kids, and they have an expectation that I'll be joining them in their homes on snow days. I've also scheduled a read-aloud during the summer and over breaks, just to keep that connection going. With modern technology, it is so much easier, and I can have it all set up in a couple of minutes, and send out emails and reminders for those who want to join in. Parents will send me pictures of their children sitting in front of the screen as I read stories over the computer. I've even gone to students' homes and done live readings from their living rooms.

Putting on this HAT: Building relationships and connecting with our kids is so important, but more importantly, I get refreshed and energized when I get time to see the kids laughing and enjoying time together. We must be creative when times are tough. These connections do matter and make a huge difference in how students connect with each other and with you. Find ways to connect and share your passions and joy.

Buy Their Stuff
Andrew Marotta

Sports fundraisers, donuts, scholarship donations, disaster relief, etc., etc., etc. The list goes on and on of things, organizations, students, and others who ask for money for a variety of things in school. When I first became a school leader, I couldn't believe how much I was being asked to donate. That person, that function, and so on. It was a bit overwhelming.

Then it hit me. I'm the Principal—of course, I have to buy their stuff, and I made up my mind I would buy one of everything. Keep 2–3 blank checks in my desk drawer, and, when the fundraiser request comes, I am ready. No check? Set a reminder on my phone to get the checks. As we progress on our journey of technology, I am seeing different groups using QR codes, Venmo, and other forms of electronic money transfer, making it even easier. You are supporting the kids, being generous, and showing you are invested and investing in your school community.

Putting on this HAT: Cassie Rodriguez was a senior, Class of 2021. I never knew her too well during her first couple of years, but in her senior year, I got to know her better. I learned about her family and friends, and, of course, that she wanted to pursue a career in art.

At the senior portfolio show, the seniors got to showcase their artwork and sell the ones they selected. The kids were so proud talking about the inspiration behind the work, showing off their creativity. It is an awesome night all around.

When I saw Cassie that night, she was beaming with pride. She was glowing like her artwork. When I asked her about her painting, "The Fried Egg," she shared her story about how life can be like the fried egg sometimes: overcooked, cracked, runny, scrambled, and more. We laughed when she blurted out, "I just like eggs, too!"

I told her, "I'll take it!" $75 framed and autographed. She was thrilled, but it was me who was even more thrilled. I was happy to make her a professional artist, selling her first piece of artwork to her principal. Life is about experiences, and the power of a single experience can go a long way. This story is a little more impactful than a fundraiser donation. I think of Cassie each day I gather my belongings in the kitchen before school. The Fried Egg hangs proudly in our kitchen for all to see. I thank Cassie for allowing me the opportunity to put on this HAT and for giving me the gift of a lifetime.

Cassie's take: My senior year was simultaneously the most rewarding and the most tribulation-filled academic year of high school, as most of my classmates would agree. This is the year when I applied to countless colleges, was stressed about acceptance, and began deciding the path I want to follow as a high-school graduate. It was in the art department that I was entirely in control of my creative process—I had space for myself to de-stress and create free of outside judgment. I was ecstatic when it was time for the senior art show; my work, along with my classmates', was proudly displayed in the hallway for everyone to see. I heard extremely positive feedback from my peers and would smile anytime I caught someone standing in front of my work and respectfully analyzing it. I was even more delighted when my principal, Mr. Marotta, came to speak to me about my work and why I'd created a certain piece, which I'd titled "The Fried Egg."

At the end of most days—after studying, working on assignments, seeing friends, and helping my family—I felt like an overcooked egg that was going up in flames.

It felt very rewarding to have my work acknowledged and bought by my principal. It was the first piece I'd ever sold in my art career. I will always be grateful for the lasting encouragement that Mr. Marotta gave me by putting on this memorable HAT!

A Reading Resolution
Lindsay Allen

Lindsay Allen is an English and Journalism teacher at Ballard Memorial High School in Barlow, Kentucky. She is married to her college sweetheart, Neil, and they have a daughter, Quinn, a dog, and a hamster. She has a passion for stories, spoken, written, or acted. Lindsay loves learning the stories of others. Lindsay shared this story when Andrew presented at Ballard County Schools, and BAM! It's in the book!

It all started with Facebook. As I was scanning my news feed, I came across a post from a co-worker of an image titled the "12 Challenge: 12 Months to Read 12 Books Recommended by 12 Friends." It piqued my interest. I love reading; I teach high-school English, for goodness' sake—it's in my DNA. *Loving* to read, though, is not the same as *having time* to read. I am a wife, a mother, a teacher, and I have . . . dare I say it . . . responsibilities. Sadly, reading wasn't high on my list of priorities. The "12 Challenge" seemed interesting, and it was two days before the start of the new year, so it was a perfect New Year's resolution for me.

Let's come back to that in a moment. One of the major goals of my 11th-grade English students is to read 1000 pages by the end of the school year. I break that down into 250 pages per quarter. At the end of the quarter, each student must do a "book talk" with me. It has become one of my favorite assignments. I sit down with the student and a copy of their chosen book, and we just talk. They talk to me about the book, and I ask questions to see if they truly read the book, were interested in the book, understood the book, and what they learned from the book. I have had great conversations with my students, but it is hard to truly engage in a balanced conversation when I haven't actually read the book myself.

That's where the "12 Challenge," my personal growth, and my students intertwine. My resolution is now the "12 Challenge: 12 Months to Read 12 Books Recommended by 12 Friends or Students."

I went to 12 of my students. These were students who loved reading but were also a diverse group who spanned different reading interests. One loved philosophical books; one loved murder mysteries. Another was passionate about H.P. Lovecraft and Cormac McCarthy. Some of them needed a day or two to find their perfect recommendations for me, while others were quick to give a suggestion. At the core, though, was an interest and a passion for reading. I was excited to get started, and the students appeared to be excited that I asked and that I cared.

Putting on this HAT: I'm a week from the end of February, and I am already four books in. One of these books isn't even one of the twelve. It's one another student insisted I read. The kids who know I have read or have been reading their personal recommendations check in with me on my thoughts and opinions. I often go to them during convenient times and talk to them about surprises, twists, and observations. It has not only allowed me to forge better relationships with students, but it has also re-ignited my passion for reading, improved my mental health, and allowed me a way to escape my responsibilities in a healthy, productive way. It's a win-win.

Bending the Rules
Brian McCann

Back when I first started teaching, in the late 1980s, new teachers in my building would be routinely assigned the least-desirable course load. New teachers had little voice. It was implied that we were lucky to have a job in a profession with so few openings at that time. I was the youngest teacher and the only new hire in five years.

But I was grateful to have a job—a job that I truly loved.

In my second year, my assignments included two sections of freshman English for ninth-graders who were designated in the junior high as non-college students. Although this might sound almost unimaginable today—that students were once pigeonholed based solely on middle school—back then, it was a common practice to track early and maintain these lanes.

At that time, the collection of students seemed unmotivated and disconnected from the promise of academic good fortune later in their high-school careers. I was told that this collection was the worst class to ever leave the junior high (little did I know that this mantra would be sung almost every year) and that I had my work cut out for me.

My philosophy for teaching these students who may have not always found classroom success in the past was to have high expectations for them, make their freshman English class meaningful, and have fun.

It prioritized building relationships before building relationships was fashionable.

I was warned that the toughest child in this cohort was a 13-year-old boy whose goal was to become the biggest burnout that the high school has ever known. Small, taut, angry, and sporting a heavy, black-leather motorcycle jacket, Jeremy arrived in my room with a chip on his shoulder.

His early days were quiet—he was assessing me, gauging my strengths—and, more particularly, my weaknesses—to see how far he could push me with the least amount of effort. His class met during the final period of the day, yet the energy of class seemed free from the last-period fatigue that plagues many late-day classes.

This class was not used to a lot of homework, so we were strategic in parsing out what needed to be done outside of class. The reading levels in these classes also ran the gamut from excellent readers to students who struggled with every sentence. We did a lot of reading early on, some silent and some oral, but always together so we had something in common to dissect and discuss while subtly teaching them some of the rudiments of the literature lens through which we would be looking at things this year.

Turns out that Jeremy was an excellent reader, both silently and orally, and even began to volunteer to read when he realized he was in a safe space. Not only did I thank all students who read aloud, but strategically praised them individually and collectively when I could.

Because I showed respect to Jeremy, the young man was of little problem to me. Perhaps every day was not rainbows and unicorns, but on the whole, it was a positive experience, and he was doing well with me.

Not so much outside of my class.

Jeremy was routinely in trouble in other classes, frequently disciplined by the assistant principal, and suspended from school often. He was consistent in making up missed assignments, but his absence from class became noticeable.

In these times, a daily paper attendance would be delivered by student messenger to your class mid-morning. Teachers would check their classroom attendance against the school's record and report any discrepancies. Some days, however, the class would be too busy, so I would do the cross-check at the end of the day. I might make a cursory look at who was out on any given day, but I didn't spend too much time during the official class period. I had too much teaching to do!

I noticed one day that Jeremy was present in my class during the last period, on time, and engaged. Something seemed odd to me, but I couldn't put my finger on it. It wasn't until after school that I realized Jeremy had been marked "absent" and suspended from the school's campus for that day. Thinking I would get some clarity the following day from the student, I didn't pursue it anymore. The next day, the same scenario. Student physically in class, yet marked "absent" and "suspended" on the school's attendance. So strange.

So on the third day, I innocently asked a friend of his who I also had in a study hall if Jeremy was in school today. The friend said not today because he was *still* suspended. "What do you mean *still*? He was in our class yesterday and the day before."

"Oh, he's still suspended from school. He doesn't want to miss your class."

Jeremy B., in his pursuit to become the biggest burnout in school history, walked across town to sneak into the high school so that he could attend his freshman English class. Although I knew I would be in big trouble if I didn't report this, I took my chance. It was more important to respect the relationship that had been forged during this year. I didn't report him, and he knew it.

Fast-forward some 15 years, and his son is now at the school. At an academic-award ceremony during his child's senior year, he attends to celebrate his son's success and hugs me at the end of the event. His trajectory has changed a lot since his freshman year of high school. He is married and has a successful professional career. We later connect on social media, and I share my condolences with him when his mother passes away.

I received a beautiful response from the young man, now in his 40s: "My mom loved you. You were the only teacher to reach me. It made a difference."

Putting on this HAT: Sometimes rules are guidelines and need to be bent. I don't regret not reporting that a student broke into the school to attend his English class.

Putting on another HAT: Relationships truly matter and will continue to reverberate years later. Hats off to teachers who realize their importance in their classroom and in their students' lives.

Student Takeovers
Kevin Spainhour

Kevin is the Principal at West Forsyth High School in Winston-Salem, North Carolina. A dynamic leader and dedicated educator, Kevin is the proud father of four children. He and Andrew played college basketball at Guilford College in Greensboro, North Carolina. They remain the closest of friends today.

During my tenure as principal over the past decade-plus, I started a school Facebook account when districts were hesitant about the use of social media in educational spaces. As the social-media phenomenon continued to grow, I began experimenting with multiple platforms. I quickly realized choosing your platform is critical to reaching your target audience. Want to connect with parents in 2017? Make a Facebook post. Looking to engage students in 2017, the answer is not Facebook. The landscape of how schools use social media accounts and what platforms are preferred can be debated by someone else in another book. I wish to share an activity we established at our high school to use social media to engage and promote our community.

When we first began our Instagram account in 2017, we needed our students to follow. In conjunction with our Homecoming Spirit Week, we devised a plan for one student each day to post on our school account throughout the day. Below are some ideas we shared with the selected student during that first experience.

Ideas of what to share/post:

- Everyday student activities (e.g., lunch in the cafeteria, hallway hangouts, etc.)

- Internship/Work Experiences

- Classroom activities and extracurricular activities

- Friends, family, your goals, and your aspirations

The most creative content creators are not the adults in our building. We learned that students enjoy hearing from one another, evidenced by the more-than 300 followers we gained on the first day. And we learned to trust our students. Getting past the fear of submitting our account to the voice of our students was an obstacle. Your leadership mind can be enveloped by all that could go wrong with empowering students with a school's social-media platform. Yet, once we established our takeover-agreement form (link below) and met with students individually, many of our fears subsided.

Fast-forward nearly six years, and excitement around Spirit Week in the fall gains momentum because of the IG takeovers. Students now submit an application to be selected for a takeover day. It became so popular we added the week before prom in the spring as another opportunity for students' voices to be heard.

Putting on this HAT: The selection of students for this concept is enjoyable and challenging. The goal is to obtain a wide-reaching audience. This is best accomplished by capturing students' different perspectives on school and life. Athletes and high-academic students are easy to identify. These students are also the individuals who often already have a voice within the school community.

Using social media to enhance the school profile through student voice is best achieved when unseen, under-the-radar students are provided an opportunity. As a school leader, meeting with those students to notify them of their selection to participate in the school's social-media takeover is rewarding. There is an immediate humility and boost to self-confidence in every student. And while the goal of this activity is to promote our school and engage our stakeholders, the participating students are blessed with a sense of belonging, respect, and new-found confidence.

Link to example agreement. Take it and use it in your school.

https://bit.ly/HATSTakeover

Building a Culture of Curiosity
Jeanne Muzi

Jeanne Muzi is the proud principal of Slackwood Elementary School in Lawrence Township, New Jersey. She has a passion for cultivating curiosity, for questioning, and for taking a creative approach to problem-solving skills. Jeanne is always a teacher at heart and was named the 2008–2009 New Jersey State Teacher of the Year.

Another heartfelt gift we provide to students is choosing to focus on cultivating a culture of curiosity across our learning communities . . . every grade, every classroom. Since strengthening creativity benefits every student, it requires a mindset and a skill set. When all the educators in a building collectively believe in the power of incorporating creative problem-solving and questioning activities into all the subject areas, students learn and enhance their creative-thinking skills! School communities change when they focus on thinking habits and attitudes. There are benefits to all when students learn to generate multiple answers and ideas, and come to understand that curiosity leads to action. This kind of culture helps students learn and practice collaboration, ratchets up critical contemplation, and helps students improve as active listeners and ponderers. Curiosity and creativity tend to grow in learning environments where students are taught to take intellectual risks. They have opportunities to learn and practice what it means to be open to new ideas and perspectives. Engaging and animated discussions are common in these environments, and students are encouraged to seek out connections to their lives in and outside of school. The essential abilities necessary to be competent questioners, creative problem-solvers, and analytical learners must be introduced, developed, and expanded upon from the moment students arrive at school and must continue for a lifetime. Creativity takes hold when a cross-pollination of ideas, understanding, knowledge, interests, and experiences collide. Students with flexible mindsets grow to be intellectually curious. Creative learning is memorable learning . . . It tends to stick! Where do we begin?

We can encourage our students to:

- Get comfortable with uncertainty: Students must know what to do when they don't know.

- Utilize imagination as a tool: Students must see that problems can be looked at in new ways and that there are often many solutions.

- To see mistakes and failure as a way to move forward: Students must understand that failure is never final and nothing to take personally. They must learn to stick with a problem, work hard, and persevere.

- Practice justifying answers and ideas: Students must learn to explain their thinking and have confidence in their conclusions, and be ready to alter their ideas.

We can support students as they learn to be metacognitive thinkers by:

- Modeling what it looks and feels like to "go inside your brain" and wonder, and then provide opportunities for students to practice, strengthen, and use this skill.

🎩 Making it possible for all students to become more skilled at clarifying their ideas, recognizing their comprehension (or confusion), and monitoring their connections by talking through their thinking.

🎩 Encouraging students to ask themselves questions like: Why am I doing this? What will be challenging for me? What steps should I take? Are there other solutions? What will I do if I get stuck? What am I confused about? Can I explain my thinking?

🎩 Make it a habit to pause for 10 seconds or more before calling on students to answer questions and before responding to their answers. Eliminate the need for a student to feel they must be the first one to have the right answer by giving everyone more processing time.

🎩 Build "Stop and Think" Activities into each day using tools such as:

Be a Collector: Habitually become one who gathers ideas, questions, and observations. These can be on an anchor chart, a collaborative collage, a slide show, in a journal, or as a shared document. Return to these collections often, and share them. Create collections about an author, a science unit, current events, etc. Discuss with students which questions in your collections would provide the most important information, or which ideas open up new connections, or which observations strengthen the meaning and purpose of an idea. Teach students to be their own collectors, so they can create their own Idea Journals, Chronicles of Creativity, Wonder Walls, Vision Boards, and Thinking Notebooks (which are common for successful inventors, designers, and scientists).

Thinking Spaces and Pauses: Use common areas such as hallways and entries to display an ever-changing array of thinking material, including a Masterpiece of the Month, This Week's Quote, Thinker of the Month, Riddles, I Spy posters, etc. Students spend a lot of time moving in hallways, and entering and exiting different spaces. Make sure they have lots of different things to see and think about. When the art and posters in our halls never change, what is displayed becomes invisible to the students.

Evidence, Please! Have students work as partners to discover evidence from non-book complex "texts." Objects can include photographs, artwork, newspaper articles, cartoons, poems, advertisements, commercials, etc. They can be physical items or digital examples. An educator can pull up various images on classroom devices for small groups, individuals, or as a whole-class introduction. After providing contemplation, observation, and wonder time, students stand and make a statement about their item and present supporting evidence for their assertions.

Museum Exhibition Teams: Students work together to select six different pictures (art prints, photographs, illustrations) or realia that are connected to a lesson or content area. The students then collaborate to decide how the items could be displayed in a museum exhibit. They must give reasons for putting particular images together. Students may take turns posing, answering, and discussing questions such as: What do you see? What is this? What colors do you notice first? What geometric shapes do you see? How does this make you feel? What is the first thing you think of when you look at this? Does this remind you of someone you know or a place you have been to? Does this remind you of something else you have seen? Does this tell a story? What is the mood? Why do you think this was made? Can you find some very interesting details in this that you may not see right away? Should this be placed in the exhibit? Why or why not? Students may present their exhibitions to their groups or as a gallery walk.

Putting on this HAT: We must begin planting seeds of creativity in the earliest elementary grades and build from there. When young students look at our world, they should be filled with wonder and curiosity . . . so they grow into lifelong learners.

Hats in School . . . Literally
Andrew Marotta

There has been a long-standing rule about no hats in school. No hats. Disrespectful. Old-school tradition. Don't wear hats indoors. They represent gangs. What else have we heard? Why? Why do we have this rule?

Years ago in Port Jervis, New York, the case actually went to the Supreme Court about hats in school. You can read the ruling here:

https://bit.ly/HATSinschool

In short, the ruling was you could *not* wear hats in the classroom or other academic spaces, but you could wear them in non-educational spaces. They ruled that the hats could be considered a distraction to the educational process.

I ask what's *not* a distraction to the educational process today? With cell phones in almost every kid's hands from elementary school and higher, the issue of hats in schools seems like nothing.

Putting on this HAT: I know there are varying opinions on this topic, with strong feelings on both sides. My opinion, and it is only my opinion, is to let the kids wear hats. If they are following the rules, doing well academically, and doing what they need to do, what is the issue? We do not allow the wearing of hoods because it is a safety issue. I want to see who is who, especially on the security camera, and not have earbuds in ears. No hoods, but we do allow hats. The kids and the teachers know that if a teacher requests the hats to be taken off in an academic space, that is the rule, and they are to comply.

We're trying to make schools a place where kids are excited to be as opposed to a place they can't wait to get out of. Kids want some freedoms, some expression, and hats can provide this for them. The blocking of wearing hats is just one more thing for kids to complain about in school. I want to put my energy into items like: Are kids engaged in class? What is the percentage of kids performing above grade level? How many kids are involved in an activity?

Have and create rules in school that are beneficial for all: students, staff, and the community. If a kid is learning and engaged, whether or not they have a hat on their head should not really matter.

The Principal's Office
Jay Billy

Students and teachers often see the principal's office or any office as *Off Limits* or a place of consequence that is to be avoided. In many schools, students get into the principal's office only if they've done something considered wrong or inappropriate. Unfortunately, many teachers think of the principal's office the same way *they* did as kids. The less time spent in the office, the better for most kids and adults. To be honest, I try to avoid spending too much time in the office as well. I like to be up and moving. It's unfortunate for our secretaries, who often have to page me if they want to find me or spend time looking at the building cameras to see where I might be. Obviously, there are things that are confidential and important that can be found in the office or could be seen by those who shouldn't see them, but I prefer to make the office accessible to everyone in the school.

When you walk into my office, you immediately see a library of educational books and materials that are free for all staff to borrow. You see a computer and a desk (usually messy) filled with papers and notes. The thing that most people notice right away is the pirate theme (I've embraced the *Teach Like a Pirate* mentality,) and the hats. I have a ton of hats. These are the hats I wear to greet students in the morning each day. The other thing that you'll notice immediately is that there is a small conference table with five chairs around it. Do I sometimes have meetings in my office? *Yes!* Do I sometimes have to discipline children or have restorative conversations with students? *Yes!* But really, this office, like the rest of the school, is for the kids. There are toys, games, and all kinds of fun stuff, including microphones and squishy balls. There are two full shelves of children's books that can be accessed at any time by both students and staff for reading.

Lunch with students: The school day can be busy, and sometimes it's hard to make a schedule and keep it. But, when I have time, I really like to invite students into my office and have lunch with them. In our school, they only have only 40 minutes to eat and have recess. If I find myself available, I'll run into the cafeteria and find a student or group of students and invite them into the office for lunch. Sometimes, they'll decline, but the lunchroom can get loud and chaotic, so, often, once they're comfortable, they really like joining me. I choose these students in a number of ways. It could be students who did something really nice for someone. It could be a student who has been having some behavior problems and needs a break. It could be a student who asks me beforehand if they can have lunch in my office. Once they've been in once, they realize that it can be fun, and it's kind of a reward to them. Most of the time, I'll find one or two students and then allow them to invite a friend or two. I find that more than four students at once can get crazy, so I prefer smaller groups.

When students come to my office for lunch, I'll ask them if they want music or rather just talk. Sometimes, they eat and sing (I have microphones that they use and can play music with). Other times, they'll play with the toys while eating and talking. I learn so much from our kids this way. I learn about what is going on in the classroom and the home. I learn about who their friends are and where I might have trouble. Sometimes, they try to persuade me to change things in school or create fun events for them. Most of all, it is time spent connecting. I enjoy it, and they enjoy it. Oftentimes, students will decide to stay the entire period instead of going out for recess. On indoor-recess days (because of the weather), it takes a group of students out of the chaos of the cafeteria and helps to keep things quieter in there. Other than the time, there really is no downside to making time to have lunch with your students. Even if you're not the principal, we know that these connections mean a lot, and they will serve your entire school community well in the future.

Putting on this HAT: Traditionally, the office (especially the principal's office) is a place that people try to stay away from. I contend that, if you make the office a place where staff and students feel welcome and comfortable, they will begin to see you and those who work in the office as helpers. For students, we know having trusted adults in their lives can literally save their lives. Make your workspaces and offices welcoming, and you'll see that your connections are better and that your school community becomes better, too.

Relationship Builder: An Imperfect Art
Andrew Marotta

Washington, DC, April 2022. My first 8th-grade trip to DC with middle schoolers. I am not sure who was more nervous: me, the kids, or the parents. I *did* know we were *all* nervous.

At the parent/student informational meeting prior to the trip, one of the major points I stressed with the students and parents besides not getting lost, not getting arrested, not damaging the museum, and more, was the *order of communication*. *If* something were to happen, we did *not* want the order of communication to be: student frantically calls/texts parent, the parent loses mind, posts on Facebook that something has happened, and school chaperones start hearing about it from people not even on the trip. We directed the students that they should tell an adult chaperone on the trip *first* and that we would contact the parent together.

We're off. We were having a wonderful time. Everything was going amazingly great and smoothly. Then it happened. I got the text. It was from a parent who I knew very well. She texted me someone had just stolen her daughter's food. *Whaaaat?* The group was all in the food court at the DC mall, eating quite closely together. How could this be?

I located her daughter, Olivia, at one of the tables and ran to her quickly. She was crying and explained that a strange woman had walked up to her, asked for a bite, and then just took the slice out of her hand. *What?* I couldn't believe it.

Immediately, my team:

- Located security and pointed out the woman.

- Went to the pizza place and explained what happened. They very generously gave her another slice.

- Called Mom and assured Olivia all would be okay.

- Had Olivia stay with the team for a little while.

I then texted Mom this picture below:

Putting on this HAT: What do you see in this picture? Pause reading for a moment and take a look at the picture. This quick text went a long way with Olivia and her parents. The picture shows:

- Presence: I was there with her, and she was okay.

- Empathy: My face shows I was sad for her and sad that this occurred.

- It will be okay: I shared with Mom that we got her another slice and that she would eat closer to the adults from now on.

- A hug: I had my arm around her. I comforted her like I would my own daughter. I know we are in the age of "Do not put your hands on kids in any way," yet this was different. She needed a hug and reassurance that this was all going to be okay.

She had been crying but was not anymore: She was on the way back to being herself.

Relationship building and trust can be a lot of different things. In a matter of minutes, this parent went from being extremely upset and concerned to feeling reassured and confident her daughter was in good hands. A picture says 1000 words, and this picture hit the spot. Be authentic in your actions and your HATS. They can mean a lot to stakeholders, in good times and bad.

CHAPTER 5

ALL HATS WELCOME

Family Fridays
Jay Billy

When the pandemic arrived in 2020, it not only brought our classroom quickly into homes, but it also brought many of our homes into classrooms. We learned things about our families and their home life and culture that we may not have known. It was a real learning experience and something I found very valuable. So, when it was time to allow people back into our schools safely, I asked each classroom teacher to find ways to invite each family into the classrooms. Whether it was to share culture or tradition, be part of a lesson, share exciting jobs, or just read a children's book that is beloved by the family, we want our families in our school.

When we talk about how children should feel that they belong and are welcome in our schools, we also mean the family. Students light up when their parent arrives to read a story or share a tradition or skill. Every student feels more like they belong when their whole family is included in what we do. Many districts have goals related to equity and belonging. This helps bolster our connections with the students and their families. In fact, in my opinion, bringing our families into the classrooms is one of the most inclusive and welcoming things we can do.

Some teachers really embraced my challenge to bring parents and family members into their classrooms, and they started calling it "Family Fridays." Others just reached out to families and scheduled them in for whenever it was convenient. The staff accepted the challenge and began scheduling family members to come in and share. Some of the families even offered various other family members to come and share their work or help with projects that highlight the traditions and jobs that their family celebrates and are part of our bigger community. Teachers even started having "Mystery Readers" come in to read their favorite family stories. These "readers" included older siblings who are in our school or in other schools in the district.

At the elementary-school level, kids are not embarrassed by their parents and are very proud of them. What little kid isn't excited to share what their parent does or fun things they do at home? When we celebrate our families, their jobs, and traditions at younger ages, it will become more welcome and accepted as students get older. While middle school and high school students may seem not to want their families involved in the schools, many may secretly feel a sense of pride as their parents share about their families.

Putting on this HAT: It doesn't have to be Friday. Any day that you invite your families into the school, you are building a sense of belonging for your students. There is comfort and acceptance of who each student is as an individual and acceptance of them as part of their family. When we build an inclusive community, we are saying that everyone is welcome and a positive contributor to our school. Remember, the next step in inclusivity is welcoming.

Becoming the Mayor
Brian McCann

Audrey entered high school as a child who lived with her profound learning disabilities and was part of a substantially separate high-school setting. By the time she graduated, she had become our town's celebrated Student of the Year.

What impressed our community the most about Audrey was how she blossomed. She was excellent on the social level, with emphatic greetings by name to her teachers and fellow students. She carried herself with confidence in the hallways and was able to integrate into mainstream classes as her high-school year progressed. Audrey thrived in our childcare program and became a role model for other students.

At open house and parent-teacher conference events, Audrey was not shy in asking those in attendance to support her childcare program's bake sale. Her direct solicitations to adults most likely netted the most money at each of these evening events.

Her teachers knew to encourage her and gently guided her when she did not recognize social cues from others. This partnership helped hone an inclusive culture in the building. By her senior year, Audrey was a social force in the hallways and the classroom.

Audrey was nominated by the school as the town's Student of the Year. She ultimately was selected and gave a speech to the community during an outdoor ceremony over a warm Memorial

Day weekend. She was honored as well in the annual Memorial Day Parade.

Audrey never gave up as a student or used her disability as an excuse. She learned how to navigate the tricky high-school road and ultimately emerged as a leader in the school, especially with her peers in the childcare program.

Equally as important, she was a catalyst in helping the entire school population recognize the benefits of a truly inclusive culture and how those reverberations of acceptance and kindness have a ripple effect throughout the school's campus.

Putting on this HAT: This model student is the product of a community. Her teachers and family outside of school proved to Audrey the benefits of trust and risk-taking during these character-building secondary years.

Saying *Yes* to Equity
Jay Billy

One thing that brings me joy about my school and district is the diversity of our families. According to the most recent census on public schools, 59 percent of our students are "minority" students. This means that we have a minority-majority . . . if that makes any sense. Over the years as an administrator, I've continued to educate myself on important issues related to race and equity in education. I've worked hard to hire a more diverse staff and make sure our students have the opportunity to see themselves in those who teach them. We've worked hard to provide our students with materials that are sensitive to race and culture so they can see the "window and mirrors" in the curriculum.

Whether your school is diverse or not, it is important that students and staff feel welcomed and included. There are many things we can do on our journey toward equity and diversity. Some are easy, and others take more work. It's easy to allow our families and students to share their cultures by recognizing and celebrating the many different holidays of our families. In our school, students share their traditions through posters, parent visits, and often through food. We celebrate the many cultures by having multicultural dinners, where food is brought into the cafeteria, and we have an evening of love and sharing. When people come together to share their differences and their similarities, we become more of one "family." We set up a student-made display of posters where the families can see the different ways everyone celebrates. This is one of my favorite nights of the year.

Another thing that our district began was having what we call "Equity Champions" at each school. These teacher-leaders are the ones who share resources, books, and articles, and even lead meetings with a focus on equity. They are paid a small yearly stipend for their work, but it ensures that we have people in each building who are making sure that our resources and instruction represent the values of our community. While we hope that all of our teachers and staff are "Equity Champions," having these teacher-leaders has ensured that very important conversations continue to happen in our school and for our kids.

I send out a newsletter each week to our families. Since we have such a diverse population, it is important that we are sharing information in a way that all families can access it. An easy way to do this is by using the Smore.com app. Smore not only allows the easy design of your newsletter as you send out information, but it also has a translation feature that includes more than 90 languages. This means that all of your families can access the information that you are sending out, which is important if you want them to feel welcome and valued.

Like many districts, we continually look at our disaggregated data to see where we need to improve. We were discussing the data at a faculty meeting one day because we noticed that many of our students of color, especially our Black students, were struggling in math. We try to have honest discussions in our meetings because we really want to look deeply at how we can help our students. Someone said that it seemed like many of our Black families don't feel as connected to the school, so they are less involved. This stuck with me and caused me and many others to ponder the reasons. One of my teachers, Erika Smoots, who is Black and has had children in our district, suggested we ask this question to our Black Families. Of course, I said, *"Yes!"* With her leading the way, we began our first Black Family Group, which later became the Black Education Advancement Council (BEAC.) The first thing Erika did was invite every one of the Black families in our school in for dinner. We scheduled an evening in our cafeteria where our Black Families came together to eat and talk. It was amazing, and I felt so humbled by the turnout and enthusiasm. After eating and talking, we asked about getting more parent involvement and how we could help. What came of this night was that Erika and many of our teachers created two evenings where parents came with their children to learn to play math games and learn more about the curriculum. It was as simple as saying "Yes" and then finding ways to help. The BEAC has grown into its own entity and supports the entire district.

It now has regular meetings with our superintendent and shares updates on social media.

Putting on this HAT: Heartfelt acts must be inclusive and must be the right thing for all who you serve. Stepping into the un-comfort zone when creating schools that welcome all is never the wrong thing to do. Most importantly, saying *"Yes"* to the ideas and creativity of those you work with will continue to help all of us grow and feel more welcome in the places we spend a large portion of our time. Say *"Yes!"* to inclusion and equity. Say *"Yes!"* . . . and *"How can I help?"*

You Matter/We Care
Mindy Milavsky

Dr. Mindy Milavsky is the proud Principal of Lawrence Middle School in Lawrence Township, New Jersey, also known as LMSNation. She prides herself on being front and center in all that happens in her school.

As a young teacher in the early '90s, I was fortunate to be mentored by some extraordinary educators. They taught me many things, the most important lesson being that happy teachers make happy kids. When I transitioned to administration, I truly understood the importance of that statement. For the past 20 years, *Happy Teachers Make Happy Kids* has been at the forefront of my leadership practice and an important part of my decision-making process.

A positive culture and climate of a school are essential in helping students and teachers learn and grow. This type of environment starts with its staff and their support of the core values of the school community. As a building leader, I have tried to create an environment where my staff is willing to take risks, build relationships with each other and their students, collaborate about teaching and learning, and are committed to the mission and vision of our school. Most of all, I want my staff to enjoy what they do.

The care and concern of our school building initiates our positive school culture and sets the stage for the success of our staff and students. As a school, we pride ourselves on greeting each person as they enter the building with a good-morning greeting, a smile, a high-five, and, on some occasions, bubbles, music, or disco lights. Pictures of students can be found on banners around the school, positive quotes are displayed throughout, bulletin boards showcase student work, and character-trait flags hang in the hallway. Cardinal Code (Be Respectful, Be Responsible, and Be Ready) expectation plaques can be found in each classroom. The school building is bright and clean.

Heartfelt Acts for teachers, students, and staff are multifaceted at Lawrence Middle School. It's a feeling you have when you walk through the hallways. It's the high-fives, applause, and laughter heard in classrooms, on the athletic fields, in the cafeteria, and onstage. It's the look on a student's face when they realize they are successful. It is the ear-to-ear smiles during house relays, minute-to-win-it, and spirit days. It's the excitement of checking out a great book from the library. It's the beautiful gratitude card you received from a student. It's the enthusiasm generated by a school-wide bingo game. It's the joy of taking part in a club or after-school activity. It's the exhilaration of competing on a team or participating in the musical. It's the acknowledgment of staff in our weekly emails. It's food deliveries to families. It's positive phone calls home. It's utilizing the Nurtured Heart Approach© and recognizing the greatness we all possess. From yearly school themes, instructional houses, activities, assemblies, community involvement, daily meditation, school celebrations, recognitions, and coursework—student and staff well-being is at the core of it all.

In order to create this type of environment, we engaged in committee work, professional development, and lots of conversations. We wanted our staff and students to be seen and heard. These conversations helped us transform the culture of our school. It led to us branding ourselves as *LMS Nation*. This was a bold statement and a new beginning. This brought us together and propelled us to achieve our goals.

It is imperative to involve staff in the daily operations of the school community. Staff in our building take on many different roles. They serve as classroom teachers, mentors, coaches, club and activity advisors, after-school supervisors, academic leaders, and collaborative colleagues. Time is allocated at the end of each day for staff to collaborate. Informal groups have been established in academic disciplines, teacher partnerships, and instructional houses. Teachers share best practices and creative ideas. Professional development is not limited to instructional practices but focuses on self-care and wellness. Our current bell schedule is a result of teacher feedback regarding the rigor of their workday. The schedule now provides an eighty-two-minute planning period that allows teachers to plan lessons, collaborate with each other, and confer with school counselors as well as parents and guardians. The simple reallocation of office space has provided our staff with a comfortable and relaxing space to share ideas, have lunch together, and enjoy their colleagues' company. Staff gravitates to this space inside our library when they need time to connect or disconnect.

Student and staff happiness starts with a sense of belonging. All students and staff are assigned to one of three instructional houses. Students remain in their house structure during their entire middle-school career. Our instructional houses generate school spirit and pride, and have helped to create traditions that everyone in our school community looks forward to each year. Students are able to develop supportive relationships with caring educators who are committed to their students and their unique instructional and social needs. By following a modified block schedule, our students receive the benefits of maximum instructional time while incorporating team-building activities, enriching assemblies, and celebrations of academic success. Students instantly are part of a team that requires them to engage in yearlong school-community activities. From wearing their house shirt on school spirit days to participating in house relays, house events, and contests, students and staff feel part of the team as they compete for the coveted House Cup. House Leaders meet with students to encourage positive behaviors which reflect our *Cardinal Code*—to Be Respectful, Be Responsible, and Be Ready.

We celebrate our staff on a consistent basis. The first thing in our weekly Sunday email is shoutouts to staff highlighting their leadership and involvement. We honor staff and students during our weekly star ticket drawing, selecting teachers alongside our star students to receive donuts and pretzels. During the month of February, we ask students to recognize their teachers with a heart award. Students submit the names of their teachers and write a short paragraph about how that staff member has improved their educational experience. Staff receives a copy of the form at the end of the month. During faculty meetings, we take a few minutes to write a note of appreciation to a staff member or share aloud a positive contribution from a colleague.

Teachers compete in house contests alongside students. These monthly staff contests/spirit days encourage collegiality amongst the staff, which fosters a fun competitive environment. A staff activity that has now become a tradition at Lawrence Middle School is the annual elf hunt. This is not just a regular treasure hunt. Paper elves are created using every staff member's face and hidden around the school. Some elves are in plain sight; others are well hidden. During the school day, staff search the building to find the elves in order to receive a prize. Staff must identify their elf and pose with their elf for a picture before a prize is issued. This activity brings laughter and tears of joy as they find an elf in the copy machine, on a random bulletin board with someone's family photos, in the snack machine, on the bathroom mirror, or amongst the library stacks. Staff proudly pose with their elf and prize in hand. The hunt is something that every teacher talks about and looks forward to; many plan their strategy prior to "Go Time."

Like many schools, we start each school year with a theme that will guide us throughout the year. As a staff, we proudly wear the theme on brightly colored staff shirts. This yearly tradition has become a highlight for our staff on the first day back in September. They are eager to see the color of the shirt and what our mantra will be. School themes such as Reach for the Stars, You Matter, We Care, Be a Cardinal, Anything Is Possible, Connected, Catch the Energy Release Your Potential (FISH Philosophy), and One Nation have guided us throughout the school year. It's not just about the shirt—it's about what it stands for. Our staff shirts provide us with a sense of pride in who we are and what we can accomplish, the shirts symbolize our collective efficacy, and the shirts remind us of our purpose.

The second tradition we started on the first day back in September was visiting students at their homes. In an effort to welcome students back to school, our entire staff has boarded buses to surprise students with a visit. Imagine 60+ teachers arriving at your home all dressed the same, singing and cheering for you. Another year we boarded the bus and dropped off teams of teachers in the neighborhood with addresses. Each team was charged with visiting five homes. Staff was equipped with pom-poms, music, banners, and lawn signs in order to welcome students back to school as the bus circled around the neighborhood, spreading cheer. One year, teams of staff were sent out on a treasure hunt to visit different parts of the community and take pictures to post on social media. First, they had to make team posters. Then they visited elementary schools and took pictures with teachers, staff members, and mascots. Next, they visited local restaurants and businesses to greet community members. Once they returned to school, they used chalk on the front walk to celebrate the first day back to school with colorful pictures and positive sayings. While some team members worked on the front walkway, others were charged with making phone calls to new students and families. The treasure hunt experience and visits to the community have helped our staff get to know each other and learn about students and the community. These activities have fostered a sense of community for our school.

Putting on this HAT: Heartfelt acts for students and staff start with being the best versions of ourselves. How we show up each and every day for ourselves and each other matters. I found this sign on one of my teacher's doors that says it best: *STOP! Before you enter this space, remember there are tender souls inside, people young and old, full of potential, who need your guidance, love, and attention. Proceed with caution!* Now more than ever, we must lead with love and care. It isn't always easy, but it is definitely worth it.

To learn more about Lawrence Middle School, you can reach out to Mindy Milavsky, Principal, mmilavsky@ltps.org or check us out on Facebook, Instagram, or Twitter: @LMSNation.

Alex #1—Transcending Disability
Brian McCann

Alex arrived at our school a month after the school year officially started. He was one of the first students in a brand-new program for autistic students who formerly were educated outside of the district instead of with the students they might have grown up with. It was a new idea for my district, and I was nervous. I had no formal training with autistic students but used a tried-and-true philosophy I use when dealing with most new initiatives I know little about.

My strategy: just be nice to the students and leave decisions to the professionals in the program.

Alex arrived about 30 minutes after the official start of the school day in a special van. The van pulled up to the front of the school and started to honk its horn, thus beginning a perfect storm in the main office.

Literally, there was no one around.

No assistant principal. No lead teacher. No roving teacher in the hall. No secretary at the main desk.

Just me. Just the principal who then physically left the building to explain to the driver about the designated drop-off spot. I decided to formally welcome the student at the same time.

"Welcome to Case High School, Alex," I heartily exclaimed. "I'm Mr. McCann, your new principal."

"Mr. Principal," he smiled and exclaimed.

"Yes, I'm the principal. I hope you have a great year here, Alex."

"Mr. Principal!" he exclaimed again.

I smiled. *Boy, are you awesome*, I thought. Not only are you greeting the new student and personally riding in the van with him to model the correct arrival spot, but your leadership has transcended his disability and he knows *just* who you are.

We arrived at the back of the building and were met by the lead teacher. I walked with him through the school doors and wished him a terrific first day.

"Mr. Principal!" he responded.

Putting on this HAT: A new student's first day at any level is a scary experience. As a school leader, try to carve out a few minutes to personally welcome them into school, spend some time getting to know them, and check in with them once in a while during these first few days. This was my plan with Alex . . . until something didn't seem exactly what I had envisioned.

Alex #2: A Magic Kingdom
Brian McCann

In my mind, I was the hero principal with Alex. A warm, personalized greeting with a new student on his first day of school, with the student—who struggles with communication because of his disability—understanding the importance of my role in the building when he first met me.

"Mr. Principal!" he exclaimed for a final time when I left him with the lead teacher to begin his school day and high-school experience in this building.

My moment of humility came on Alex's second day.

I went upstairs to his program's room ready to be greeted once again with full recognition of my school leadership in concert with the positive relationship I was forging with this child.

"Good morning, Alex."

"Hi, Birdie Bird Brain."

Huh??? I looked around. No one seemed to notice this strange appellation in the room, except for the lead teacher, who immediately busied himself with something on his desk.

I didn't know how to react. So I did the principal thing: I just pretended I didn't hear it and went on with my day.

Day 3: same title. Day 4: same title.

Finally, at the end of the week, I was debriefing about the week's successes and struggles with the lead teacher when I finally got up the courage to ask. Why "Birdie Bird Brain"? What happened to "Mr. Principal"?

The teacher—who had studied the student's IEP and case history—shared with me that Alex often identifies people in the room with Disney characters. At present, he identifies with the character of Dumbo, even to the point of carrying a small Timothy Mouse stuffed animal with him. Oftentimes, Alex will do a brief assessment of the person he is interacting with and provide them with a Disney name.

Alex also had a detailed knowledge bank of all things Disney. There is a hierarchy: elephants are the most revered of his titles. This was sometimes hard to accept when a young woman entered the program room for the first time, but a little pre-warning usually assuaged the situation. He favors animals and princesses, but on occasion presents people with a Disney allusion to a character we may have forgotten about. My assistant principal at the time, for example, was referred to as "ICHABOB," which was a reference to the cartoon characterization of Ichabod Crane and the headless horseman of Sleepy Hollow.

I have to admit, I googled a picture of Disney's Ichabod Crane and immediately thought, "Now that you mention it, Ichabod does look a lot like. . . ."

Not too soon after that, I had to spend some time in the classroom and observe some of the individual skills and projects the students were working on. Alex greeted me as Birdie Bird Brain. No one smiled or laughed. Knowing that I might not get the answer I was searching for, I asked this anyway.

"What movie can I find Birdie Bird Brain in, Alex?"

He blinked. "Melody 1953," he responded and returned to his computer.

Instantly I recall a Disney VHS tape in the old-school plastic clamshell that my oldest daughter had in the late 1990s called "Melody Time." I thought to myself that Alex was confused about the title.

This caused another round of humility for me.

That night, I took out my iPad and searched for "Melody Time" and "Birdie Brain."

This is what I did find. Let me first preface that Alex was 100 percent correct.

"Melody" is a 1953 Disney short cartoon in which Professor Owl teaches music fundamentals to his students, including one called "BERTIE BIRDBRAIN." Another Google search produced the cartoon character's picture. Copyright prohibits me from recreating here, but Google "Bertie Birdbrain Melody 1953 Disney," and a Technicolor image of me as seen through Alex's eyes will emerge.

My wife agreed that the image was uncanny and Bertie's dunce cap apt, given this situation.

Alex might be autistic and lives each day with a communication disability that limits his interaction with people, but he taught me a valuable lesson that day.

Putting on this HAT: Professor Owl in 1953's "Melody" is described in Wikipedia as instructing "his class of birds on how to find the melody around them." Do not underestimate the knowledge base of all your students. Each one has a special niche that you, as an educator, should seek to uncover during their journey with you. His acute power of observation and how to find a parallel to an animated world he is passionate about is truly a gift.

Alex #3: Reaping the Fruit of Kindness
Brian McCann

Alex brought a smile to me each day. He was always happy, seemed interested in the tasks at hand, and always greeted me with "Hi, Bertie Birdbrain." I'm certain other students heard him, but I never heard that moniker used by other students.

Alex did well in his academic classes, went on many field trips where he worked in a variety of capacities in the community, and participated in school events, like the annual pep rally. All of his high-school ventures were with the companionship of his small Timothy Mouse, which he carried with him at all times.

When Alex was going to be part of the June graduation ceremony, I surprised him onstage with a small diploma for Timothy Mouse. From the effusive email I received from his family after the event, not only did they appreciate the personalized journey that Alex was on at this high school, but it was evident that many adults in the community knew their students.

He didn't say much. Other than my daily greeting, he may echo a word or two from whatever statement he last heard. He was gifted in finding the Disney doppelganger for any visitor to his program, but other than discovering your cartoon equivalent, he was a young man of few words.

Alex stayed at the high school until his 22nd birthday. A few days before his scheduled departure date, his program put together a "slide show" of Alex at our school over the years. Each picture was filled with happiness. I was asked to say a few words before the cake was served.

I'm not usually lost for words, but I couldn't get many out that afternoon. My throat constricted, my eyes welled up, and my voice began to crack. *Who looks like a birdbrain now?* I thought to myself. Although overcome with emotion, I was authentic in my fondness for this student.

On his last day, I ventured up to his program to wish him the best of luck in his new adult program that would start soon. I also wanted to shake Timothy Mouse's hand for the last time. I braced myself in preparation that I would again be too emotional and decided that a quick exit was the best for me. Alex was seated at a computer.

Just wish him well. Shake Timothy's hand. Give him a pat on the back. Exit swiftly and gracefully.

Yet, my intentions were thwarted. He turned to me and looked me right in the eyes.

"I'm going to miss you, Bertie Birdbrain," Alex said in his final words to me.

Stunned, I returned to my office. This young man whose disability made communication difficult for him gifted me with the longest sentence I have ever heard him say. I sat in my office chair, unable to move, once again on the verge of tears. I hoped that his next placement was a world of kindness and love, as this high school had been for Alex.

A couple of summers later, I was in the post office mailing some official notices for the school. I saw Alex from a distance. He looked the same and was flanked by Timothy Mouse once again. His face lit up when we passed each other.

"Hey, Alex."

"Hey, Bertie Birdbrain."

I was never so happy to hear that title once again. We didn't stop and chat or catch up with his family. We simply shared a moment that paid tribute to the relation-  ship forged between principal and student a few years back.

Putting on this HAT: Relationships truly matter. It's the time that you spend getting to know your students—*all* of your students—that results in big payoffs. Some students may not understand what your title means, but they know when someone is kind, cares about them, and is truly interested in their success. Kindness can transcend disability in many instances. Alex is merely one example.

The Delaware River Run
Andrew Marotta

I watched the *30 for 30 Sports Center Feature* entitled "17 Hours" on ESPN. It highlights Chris Nikic's story of completing an Ironman competition with his father. What makes it special is that Chris is the first person with Down syndrome to complete an Ironman. It was a beautiful and heartwarming story. It moved me and touched my spirit.

As I ran on the elliptical, I reflected on the amazing accomplishment of not only Chris but also his Dad. His Dad was dedicated to making his work, training alongside his son, being there for him, and more.

I began to think—*What can I do for my students in my school? Could I provide an opportunity to some amazing kids in my school like this? Like Chris did? An Ironman? That would be a bit much for a principal to lead his students, but how about a 5K?*

In Port Jervis, New York, each spring, the recreation department, led by Mr. John Faggione, puts on the Delaware River Run, a 5K that literally runs right through the campus and the town. It is on a Sunday morning, and it is just perfect.

Why couldn't I run this race with my students? Bam! We got together and gathered the students' interest. Whether running, walking, doing part of the race, giving out water, or cheering on the runners, all the students were excited to be part of it.

We put together a training schedule and exercise regimen and got to it.

Putting on this HAT: Why not? Why couldn't our kids do it? Their learning disabilities and some of their physical challenges **would not stop them**. Their spirit, teamwork, and excitement for the event were just awesome. They're amazing, and they've inspired me to be a better leader.

It is March at the time this book is being submitted for completion and the race is in May. I know it will be a special event that I hope will grow and become an annual tradition. I'd like to thank each one of these awesome student-athletes, their families, their teacher, and their assistants for the courage to take on this challenge. Port Pride all the way! #GoPort #TwoClaps

CHAPTER 6

HATS . . .
THEY ALL MATTER

Poker

Jay Billy

We like to have fun at our school, so I'm continually trying to come up with ways to keep our staff and teachers
engaged and taking risks. One simple way to engage the entire
staff throughout the day is to create challenges. One challenge I
thought of is Poker.

How Poker works on a school-wide level is this. When the building is empty, I take a regular deck of cards and walk through the
building, hiding cards in plain sight or slightly covered. I usually
don't hide them in classrooms or bathrooms because I want everyone
to have a fair chance. Then, I'll send out an email at night, telling
everyone that we are playing Poker the next day. I remind staff that
there are 52 cards hidden throughout the building and whoever has
the best Poker hand at the end of the day, will win a gift certificate.
Usually, I buy a gift card to Starbucks or a local bakery to sweeten
the incentive, but some of the staff are so competitive that I don't

think I even need to have a reward. I also make sure that I share the rules of Poker and the ranking system of hands so that even those who aren't familiar with playing cards can participate.

As staff arrives the next day, they are more aware as they walk through the building. Some even come earlier than usual, just so they have time to look for cards. They begin accumulating cards and building their Poker hands. Sometimes, they will share what they have with others and trade cards, trying to get the very best Poker hand. By the end of the day, usually I have three or four staff members who have hands they think may be winners. They'll bring them to me, and I'll hand out the reward to the winner. As I mentioned, we have some staff members who are quite competitive, but it is just a fun time, looking for cards, working to get the best hand, and trying to out-think or bluff others into trading for other cards or hands.

Putting on this HAT: Continue to think of ways to engage your staff in things that bring them together, get them to talk, and show them that school can be a place of fun. You don't have to have all of the ideas; you just have to say "Yes" when staff comes up with ideas for fun and excitement in the school. Challenges are a good way to keep everyone on their toes, engaged with each other, and staying connected with the entire school community. You don't have to spend a lot of money or time, and, once you play, everyone knows the game and wants to play again the next time.

Not *Can* We, But *How Can* We?
Andrew Marotta

The pandemic presented countless problems around the world, many ongoing for years on end. One immediate problem was:

How can we run events for kids at school? The spelling bee, school dances, basketball games, graduation, and more. People were angry, frustrated, and felt the need to vent wherever they wanted. It was a rough time.

We started to ask the question: How can we? Not: *Can we,* but *how can* we? That one little word—"how"—changed the whole thing. Not *Can* we have a dance, not *Can* we have a graduation, not *Can* we have a graduation celebration, but *How can* we?

It became very freeing and liberating—an opportunity to break from the norm, have energizing brainstorming sessions, collaborate like never before, and produce some outcomes that we never thought possible.

Putting on this HAT: The pandemic was exhausting, and we're all glad it's over. Some of the positive memories remain. Here are a few highlights:

- **The individual graduations:** While the parents missed out on the big stadium graduation with all the fanfare, they did enjoy "the moment in the sun." We held individual graduations five minutes at a time. Parents could walk close to the stage, take some close-up pictures, and chat with the students for a few minutes as they graduated. Instead of the fast-moving conveyor belt of handshakes and diploma handoffs, it was more like having a cup of coffee with the students and family. Also, unplanned by us, groups of friends coordinated selecting their time slots, allowing them each the opportunity to see their closest friends graduate along with their families. It was a unique, memorable experience.

● **No indoor dances:** Fine—we schedule one outside. Can't dance within six feet of another person—we'll make chalk circles for kids to dance in . . . their own little pods. The outdoor, parking-lot dance event became a beautiful event with kids decorating their cars, hanging string lights and lamps in an otherwise nondescript parking lot. Organic chalk drawing, cornhole, and can jam, at a high-school dance. It all worked out because we asked, *"How can* we?" not *"Can* we?" While many other districts just canceled, we kept asking the question.

● **Graduation celebration:** For most years in Port Jervis schools (New York), we hosted the "All-Night Grad Party" after graduation. A bash was held in the school that ran into the wee hours of the morning (#exhausting). No all-night grad party? OK—then what can we do to celebrate our seniors? The new tradition of the graduation-celebration parade was born!

» Decorated cars, trucks, floats, and more parading through town, honking, cheering, and celebrating our seniors.
» Coordinated local radio playing songs the kids selected in all the cars and houses, so all were hearing the same music, including the graduates' names.
» Community members, families, and friends lined the streets and filled yards watching, waving, and cheering the kids.

A brand-new tradition was born, and each year it has grown into a bigger, better, and more-creative celebration. We might never have thought of it unless we **put on this HAT:** *How can we?*

Helping the Principal Be a Risk-Taker
Brian McCann

In my early years as the building principal, I feared when students would propose a new idea. Probably stemming from my insecurities in being a new building leader, I was on the fast track of perfecting the art of "NO" to new requests, especially from students.

In my limited experience, students had many ideas, but they were lacking in how to effectively plan and execute them.

I met my match with Mary Margaret.

As a freshman, she was an aggressive class president. She learned to rally her troops and led her class to Spirit Week victories for four consecutive years, titles that historically went solely to the seniors of the school.

Mary Margaret was a force of nature. She knew what she wanted, but, more importantly, tried to see what the roadblocks *might* be in front of her and thwart them before embarking on her journey.

Before her senior year, she asked to meet with me over the summer to talk about a new idea. She wanted the senior class to have an off-campus fall social at a restaurant/small banquet facility. This class president wanted to start her senior class's final year off on a positive note with a black-and-white semi-formal social.

She chose this theme because she and her officers felt that most students would have *something* to wear to a black-and-white affair and that it could be as simple or fancy as an individual wanted to make it.

She came prepared with prices, security detail, permission forms, and protocol on how the event would be breathalyzed before students entered. The president knew the calendar of fall events and carefully selected a date that would not interfere with anything school-related for one evening.

Mary Margaret also made sure that the cost was affordable for her classmates.

Basically, Mary Margaret thought of everything. She knew I would be concerned, first of all, about the safety of the students. She had a detailed plan of the entrance, where students could take pictures outside, and how a local police detail would be used that evening.

As much as I wanted to say "No," she spent time predicting my concerns and had answers to any hesitation.

Her proper planning, determination, and positive attitude during the whole process motivated me to take a chance.

Fast forward: the evening was a tremendous success. The event paid for itself, students had a great time, and I didn't lose my job over trusting a 17-year-old.

In fact, Mary Margaret set in motion an unwritten protocol that students used moving forward. She motivated the next graduating class to develop a plan for a new prom venue that included transportation via motor coaches for all.

A decade later, Mary Margaret is a successful elementary teacher. I hear from her annually and love to see how the skills she developed in high school have enhanced her current leadership in her own classroom.

Putting on this HAT: Hats off to Mary Margaret since she recognized at an early age how to be positively strategic and ultimately changed my leadership mindset from *"No"* to *"What if?"*

Deposits and Withdrawals
Jay Billy

One of the key concepts when we speak about equity is that everyone gets what they need instead of everyone getting the same thing. This equity can look quite different for each person. So, while we need general rules for our staff that are documented in the staff handbook, I feel it's important that we show the most respect for those we work with when we treat them, and each situation, with a kind heart and provide grace for what people are going through. Each year at the opening staff meeting, we discuss deposits and withdrawals. Deposits are those things that a staff member is doing above and beyond the contract that make our school and our community better places. Most people involved in education are continually making deposits into the bank of good faith, positive performance, and conscience. Withdrawals are those times when staff members need something in return that isn't necessarily part of their contract or general expectations. As school leaders, we must understand that nothing is ever black-and-white. There is a gray area that we must continually navigate in order to keep good people invested in our mission.

Deposits: If you are a school leader, you know when staff members go above and beyond in their performance. Here are some examples of staff who are making deposits:

- Someone who joins a committee or who volunteers to help outside of their contracted hours.

🎩 Someone who shows up for summer functions.

🎩 Someone who starts a club or agrees to mentor students who need something extra.

🎩 Someone who is always available to help out wherever they might be needed.

🎩 Someone who shows up for PTO/PTA meetings and events even if not required.

🎩 Someone who is continually sharing ideas and thoughts with you and doesn't mind leading initiatives.

🎩 Someone who volunteers to cover classes when you are short on substitutes.

Deposits happen all of the time, and we don't always see them, so we must be conscious of those who go above and beyond for our school and our students, and recognize these people for the extra that they bring.

Withdrawals: Here are some examples of when staff needs to withdraw from their accounts:

🎩 Someone who needs to leave a little early for a good reason.

🎩 Someone who needs to miss a staff meeting for an appointment.

🎩 Someone who needs brief class coverage of their class because they need to make an important phone call.

🐟 Someone who needs extra time to complete lesson plans, report cards, or any paperwork.

Withdrawals should happen infrequently but in good faith and are requested because someone is thinking creatively about how they can balance their personal needs and the needs of the school and community.

Although the language of "deposits and withdrawals" seems quite businesslike and less personal, it really has to do with staff members feeling that their work and efforts are being noticed and rewarded. I've had teachers come up and say to me, "I need to make a withdrawal today because I have a 3:30 doctor's appointment. Can you get coverage for my bus duty?" It really has to do with finding little ways to recognize the extra that people are putting into this work.

Putting on this HAT: There are so many ways we can recognize those who always do a little extra. Sure, everyone loves money, breakfast snacks, luncheons, etc. Mostly, people want to know that you see what they are doing and that you appreciate it. When they don't have to stress over the little things in their life because they know that you are aware of their "deposits" and that you will take care of them when they need to make a "withdrawal," people will go that extra mile for you and your organization.

Shenanigans: Staff Swap
Jessica Stokes

Jessica is a K-5 general music teacher, elementary choral director, and beginning band director at two elementary schools in the Delaware

Valley School District in northeastern Pennsylvania. In addition to being a passionate music educator, Jessica is proud to be both a wife and the mother of two daughters. She met Andrew because she was lucky enough to be the music teacher for all three of his children!

Sometimes, a little bit of shenanigans is good for a school. Sometimes, we all need to shake it up a little bit. Sometimes, school becomes a little bit stagnant for all of us. This is where the Staff Swap becomes an amazing tool for everyone!

A Staff Swap is exactly what it sounds like: All staff who are willing to participate swap places for the day. All participating staff members must leave plans for their "substitute," no one can swap places with a staff member of the same discipline or grade level, and it must remain a surprise for the students! In our building, participating members are entered into a computer-generated randomizer, such as a gift-exchange generator, to find their new job for the day. When I brought this idea to our principal the first time, he was both excited and apprehensive. When he had me introduce this idea to our staff, they thought I had completely lost my mind. Perhaps I had, but they trusted me enough to give it a try. And it was fabulous!

The benefits of a Staff Swap are innumerable for all involved. First, it truly allows staff members to "take a walk in someone else's shoes." As educators, we can become incredibly self-centered, thinking only about what we need to do, how difficult our own jobs are, and how important our specific disciplines are to our students' educations. We put on our blinders, we do our own jobs, and we forget that every one of our colleagues are hard at work, thinking the exact same things. Swapping places for the day opens our eyes to the daily tasks, joys, and struggles that our colleagues face. It allows us to appreciate the important role each educator plays in our schools and in the lives of our students.

Second, it allows us to appreciate what we do each day and to find the joy in our own classrooms again. For example, the last time we did our school swap day, I was feeling overwhelmed in my music classroom. I was overwhelmed by the sheer number of students I teach each day, the amount of noise I hear each day, and the seemingly endless preparation of my classroom instruments and supplies. Then I was swapped with the librarian. I was unprepared for the amount of books I would be reshelving, the various technologies that would be requested from me, the deafening silence of the space, and the oddness of seeing so few students in one day! I returned to my music room the following week with a renewed sense of joy for what I teach, as well as a greater understanding of our librarian's day-to-day life at school.

Finally, from the perspective of a special-area teacher, a Staff Swap can go a very long way in boosting morale and building a positive school culture. Often, special-area teachers are categorized differently from homeroom teachers. Homeroom teachers are responsible for the "core" subjects—those educational areas evaluated by standardized tests—and sometimes this reality can lead to a difficult perspective in a school: "core" subjects are important; "special" subjects are not important. This is not intentional, but it can negatively impact a school's culture. By swapping staff across the disciplines, both homeroom and special-area teachers can gain a new appreciation for each other. A little appreciation goes a very long way!

For our students, a Staff Swap is exhilarating! Can you imagine walking into your classroom to find that your fifth-grade homeroom teacher has been temporarily replaced by your physical-education teacher? Or that your kindergarten teacher is today's art teacher? Or that your history teacher is now your algebra teacher? It's weird! It's different! It means that everyone is going to have to work together—students *and* teachers—to learn and succeed. It gives a new responsibility to the students: they must become helpers and leaders in their classrooms. It allows students to see their teachers in a new light, in a new space, in a new role. Perhaps most importantly, it reveals that we are all on the same team, and we all have the same goal: to provide the best and most well-rounded education for all of our students.

Putting on this HAT: Have a Staff Swap day! Choose a day that is convenient: consider state testing dates, holidays, end of grading periods, etc. Be sure to make this voluntary; the first year might be a small swap, but it will grow. Step into a new set of shoes, change your perspective, and watch how it changes your school!

Two New Dads: A Long-Lasting Lesson in Respect
Brian McCann

You really never know what you may have in common with one of your students.

When Philip was a junior in high school, he unexpectedly became a dad. Word got out across the school hallways that Philip's girlfriend was expecting a baby in the winter.

This gossipy wildfire came at the same time that my wife and I discovered that our family was growing with our second child, also due in the winter.

Philip was my student at the time. We worked every day in our journalism elective and spent many nights at drama rehearsals together as well. I recall being in a 1990s-style computer lab one afternoon working on the school paper with students, when the people in attendance seemed to have dwindled to just Philip and me.

I took advantage of this opportunity. "Isn't it sort of a coincidence, Philip," I asked him, "that you and I are both going to be new dads real soon?"

I recall his expression as first one of surprise, and then relief. He acknowledged my question but didn't have much to add. Up through the birth of my second daughter, I don't remember too many heart-to-heart conversations with Philip about this topic. I may have asked for some updates on how mom was feeling, but I don't recall that this coincidence was at the crux of our interactions. We had a healthy teacher-student relationship. We spent time in class together and some nights working on the school's drama production.

I sort of lost track of Philip after his graduation. We would occasionally bump into each other at a restaurant and later connected on social media. It wasn't until I was going to retire from school that he truly resurfaced.

Philip was one of the highlighted speakers at my retirement party. My wife arranged for him to come to speak as a surprise to me after he sent me a beautiful congrats email earlier in the spring.

The nervous boy who had suddenly become a dad-adult had transformed into a confident public speaker. He shared with the crowd his high-school circumstance of being a new dad. He also shared our coincidence at the time. He revealed to the assembled guests that I was the only adult to acknowledge his pending fatherhood at the high school with dignity and respect. He said that I was the only teacher who would talk about what he was going through earnestly. While others might have made him the butt of a catty comment or "funny" name because of the situation he'd gotten himself into, he told my guests that I was the only one who treated a new dad who was just a boy himself with respect.

Relationships matter. Authenticity can make or break a relationship as well.

Putting on this HAT: Philip reminds us of the repercussions and the long-lasting power of kindness, that words are powerful and can help guide children through tough times. To have your impact on one child made public some two decades after he graduated was humbling. I want to think that he has paid forward this strategy to his own children, who have become adults as well.

Follow Up and Show Up
Andrew Marotta

We had a bad fight in the hallway one afternoon. Two big kids went at it, punching, kicking, etc., and crashed into the wall. I mean like really punching. Heather Heidelberg, one of our teachers, now an administrator, was on the scene quickly and helped break it up. She actually got knocked down during the altercation and still was trying to break up these two boys.

We settled the situation, sent all necessary people to the nurse, suspended the boys, wrote the referrals, and moved on. *Moved on? Moved on? What?* How could I have *moved on* so quickly? I missed the most important part of the whole situation: I failed to follow up with Heather.

Was she OK? Did she need anything? Was she injured? Did she need to be heard? What? How could I have forgotten to be there for my people, my staff literally putting their life on the line to help protect students?

It was 48 hours later that someone reminded me, "Hey, knucklehead, you probably should check on Heather!" OMG! I flew down to Heather's room and fell on my sword. I apologized profusely that I'd missed this important act: checking in on your people.

Heather was great. She was gracious, forgiving, and understanding, and we had a great conversation about supporting one another. I should have been there sooner without needing to be reminded, to listen, comfort, and check in with her.

Heather's take: I did completely understand how overwhelming the school year was (with discipline), so I didn't take it too personally, but of course, a part of me was disappointed that our building leader did not check in with me. Admitting our mistakes isn't always easy, but Andrew makes it part of a learning experience. Opening up lines of communication and just sharing my (not so great) experience was enlightening for both of us. Andrew was more aware that checking in on his teachers is crucial for maintaining positive relationships, and I learned that it's OK to let your principal know your true feelings. How else can someone improve if we don't talk about these kinds of occurrences? In the end, we both grew from the experience.

Putting on this HAT: E+R=O: Event plus response equals outcome. It wasn't the event that was the major issue—it was my failure to follow up (response) with my staff and check on my people. While the fight was a major incident, Heather was able to recover from the fight quicker than she did from my failing to check in with her to make sure she was okay.

Always take care of your people. Always follow up, and always check if there is anything else you could do. I was so caught up in the event that I failed in the most important act, which is taking care of your people. When you take care of the staff, they take care of the students.

A Robin Hood Christmas Story
Martin Geoghegan

Martin R. Geoghegan is the principal of the Henri A. Yelle Elementary School in Norton, Massachusetts. An English teacher as well as high-school and middle-school administrator, Martin also has led in the state's ASCD and school-administrator association. He is a national conference presenter, a MassCUE Pathfinder recipient, and has been honored with a 2017 Model School distinction. A father of two, he lives in Kingston, Massachusetts, with his wife.

This past Christmas, I had this wonderful story happen out of the blue, which surprised me yet made me remember the goodness of kids at any time of year.

It was a Friday afternoon, and I was trying my best to get my weekly newsletter completed so that I could head home for the weekend. I am always attempting to leave semi-early on a Friday, but it never happens. Something will inevitably happen to derail my intentions of getting out of the building and getting home.

This mid-December Friday fell into the same predicament. There I was, in my office around 4:30 p.m., working on my Smore newsletter. The phone started ringing. I begrudgingly answered it. On the other end of the line was a parent, who, sadly, I knew pretty well, because her son, Jonny, had been in trouble multiple times over the course of the year. She said to me that Jonny had come home with a $100 bill, and she was confused. I was as well.

She proceeded to tell me that a classmate of Jonny's, Raheem, had given it to him during school. I began to explain to her that, in the past, we have had students exchange money over Pokemon cards, video games, or other such 4th- and 5th-grade toys. I asked if she knew if Jonny might have "sold" something to Raheem? She said, "No," and reiterated that he just *gave* it to Jonny. Again, she was confused.

I told her I would call Raheem's parents and would also let her know what we find out and investigate on Monday, since it was so late on a Friday. I then thought I would finish my newsletter and leave that for my assistant principal to deal with on Monday.

But as I got back to work on Smore, it just kept gnawing at my brain in terms of what was this about. Raheem Senit is such a "good kid"; I couldn't think of anything nefarious that this might be, but $100 changing hands? This was very interesting. I decided to call Raheem's mom.

Raheem's mom answered the phone, and, when I told her the story that Jonny's mom had told me, she, too, was very confused. Raheem had just had a birthday and had received some money from family members, but she couldn't think of why he would bring it to school or buy something from a classmate. Mrs. Senit wasn't home at the time, but she would also check on it and give me a call on Monday; she asked if I could call her and explain it to her if I'd figured anything out after investigating.

With that behind me, I went back to work to finish the newsletter to get myself home.

Not 10 minutes later, the phone rang again, and, again, I reluctantly answered it. It was Raheem's mom. Mrs. Senit sounded upset. My mind was spinning with what she might have found out from her son.

She then relayed to me that Raheem had taken the money from an envelope they had had on their counter. The money was from a tenant they had in an apartment above their house. The tenant had put cash in an envelope with rent that they had owed them. There were months that they were short, and they had said this month they were going to try to pay off some of the money they owed them.

When Raheem's mom and dad counted the money in the envelope, they were confused, because it didn't have any extra money, but they just figured it was "that time of the year," when everyone is spending more than they would like and they weren't able to add any money.

But when Mrs. Senit questioned Raheem about my conversation with her, he explained to his mom that Jonny talked about in class how he wasn't looking forward to Christmas and that this was "going to be a horrible time for him and his family." Raheem thought that his family "had all they needed" and that they would enjoy Christmas even without the money he could give Jonny to make his holiday just that much better. Mrs. Senit was crying by the time she got to the end of the story. She said that Raheem shouldn't have stolen the money from them, but she so appreciated his caring heart.

I was so shocked by all I had just heard. I knew Jonny's situation and knew that his name was definitely on the list of kids we were supporting during the holiday season, but Raheem's actions were just so fabulous. He is such a great kid. He cared so much and wanted to share what his family had to brighten up his friend's holidays.

I told Mrs. Senit how awesome a friend Raheem was and how I would get the money back on Monday from Jonny's mom and have it back to them. She then stopped me and said, "Oh, no, you won't, Mr. G. You will make sure they have that $100 and ask if there is anything more the Senits could do to help them." God bless awesome people!

I again told Mrs. Senit how great a family they are, and how we can realize where Raheem gets his awesomeness from. I then called back Jonny's mom to tell her about how she needed to keep the money. I then had my second mom on the phone way after hours on a Friday, crying, for all the right reasons.

We did a #GoodNewsCallOfTheDay for Raheem on Monday, where he explained to me how he knew stealing was wrong, but again, where we talked with him about how he is such a caring, generous, and kind person, and how he should never let that part of him go. When we called Mr. and Mrs. Senit for the #GNCOTD, they again asked if there was anything more they could do for Jonny or any other students like him. Awesome!

Putting on this hat: When we are administrators, we sometimes go to the negative of a situation without thinking about how there might be a positive influence as to *why* an incident occurred. It is just part of the job. We are hit with so many gloomy circumstances that our mind sometimes goes to them, when we need to think openly about a scenario and how there might have been a more optimistic reason *why* something happened. This is what this story clearly illustrates. In past situations with the exchanging of money, it always was a bleak story, but here, it was a Robin Hood-type of goodness that shone through.

Out in Front Every Day
Brian McCann

Recently, I was asked at an interview what would be one non-negotiable in my school day. Given how a school's daily climate can shift on a dime, there are not many things we can call "certain" outside of the day beginning at exactly a certain time and ending at the last bell. Despite all plans and provisions, we cannot wrangle and control everything in between.

I did not hesitate in my non-negotiable. I will welcome children to the school in the front of the building each morning. I will greet them repeatedly and add their name when I can.

I will not defer to rain, cold, heat, or wind. I can find a hat, some gloves, and an umbrella, if necessary.

I will be in front for the first bus, and I will remain until the final bus disembarks.

I will then transition to the student parking area to greet those who drive (or are driven) to school.

Students, teachers, and families will know where I am for the first 20 minutes of each school day, at least before the formal day starts.

Children will hear kind words from me and begin their day at my school with the word "*good.*"

I will not assign this as a duty to my assistant. I will not pay a professional to greet children. I will not think of checking my email before school as something more important. I will call people back who choose to contact me at this time later in the morning.

I will be the face of the high school at the onset of each school day. I will smile and offer praise and encouragement. I will congratulate someone who played last night, performed in the chorus of a musical over the weekend, or was celebrated recently in traditional or social media.

I will welcome back the student who was sick yesterday and tell that child that we missed him or her.

Behind my smile and ubiquitous greetings, I will conduct a welfare check on each student I see. Is something different today? Why did that child avoid my gaze? What happened so that the student's arm is in a sling? As a building leader, do we ever really know what has happened to a child the morning prior to school or the night before? Isn't this time crucial to gauge if some change may have occurred?

I shivered when I heard a story once about how a student in another state was on the verge of making a bad, hurtful, and calamitous decision involving the school community. Although obviously in great pain, this student said that he/she would follow through with this negative action *unless* someone spoke to them directly during the school day. That sad scenario stayed with me for years.

Putting on this HAT: From this scenario, I choose to wear the same hat each morning. I will greet my school to the greatest extent possible each day. For some, mine will be the first voice heard in the day, and it will be filled with love and positivity . . . even when I might be vulnerable and having a rough start.

Show Me the Money
Casey Hallgarth

Casey Hallgarth is the superintendent of the beautiful small school district of Prairie City, Oregon. Casey and his beautiful wife, Heidi, have two sons, Quinten and Cameron. Casey's strength comes from his grandparents, who raised him and gave him his values and character as a man. He knew no other way but to listen to his grandparents. Casey: Have you ever tried talking back to your grandma? Not me!

Wow, that school's gym looks like a college gym! What size school is this? 1A . . . how does a small school in rural Eastern Oregon have one of the best 1A gyms in Oregon? They must have some rich ranchers and farmers who donate to the school, right? Nope.

Many schools struggle with basic maintenance care for their buildings. Some schools don't have any extra carryover in the budget, and, if they did, shouldn't that go to the fund of some after-school programs or to help the teachers and staff? What's the answer to getting a college-style gym without breaking the bank? Action—and vision.

I took a writing class in college focused on grant writing. The book we had to purchase was "Grant Writing for Dummies." My first thought was, *You've got to be kidding . . . really?* Turns out I didn't learn too much from that class on writing grants, but, more importantly, I learned the formula for being a successful grant writer. You must accept that you won't get every grant you apply for, but, with action, you will keep going after them until you get one. I have gone after most of our grants because of someone sharing the information or because I just get curious and start googling ideas for grants.

Putting on this HAT: Everyone thinks that you need to have some magical skill to get a grant, but, really, all you need is a reason. I am a dreamer, a visionary who loves to daydream about what we can do to be the best in the state in all facets of our school district. These dreams and visions are contagious to the community. Our small community loves our gym so much that we have held wedding receptions, funerals, and even donkey basketball games, to name a few activities. The bottom line is to see your vision or dream and make it your reason to go out and find that grant to help your school.

Morning Announcements
Christopher Turnbull

Christopher Turnbull is the principal at Bear Tavern Elementary School in Hopewell Township, New Jersey. Chris was named the 2022 Visionary Principal for the State of New Jersey and is currently in the process of finishing his Doctoral program at Rider University.

While morning announcements can seem mundane and normal, they can be a vehicle every day to spread joy and enthusiasm, while explicitly teaching kindness, empathy, and teamwork.

The evolution of our morning announcements began five or so years ago when we used a canned program that had a daily script and always ended with "Make it a great day or not—the choice is yours . . ." Over time, some of the celebrities who were quoted had fallen from grace, and the structure became a bit stale. So, we started our own version, using the loudspeaker. We would still announce birthdays and important information, but we'd also introduce a quote of the week on Monday to create a character tie-in. On Tuesday, we'd dive into the quote a little bit deeper; on Wednesday, we'd break down the person who said the quote; on Thursday, we'd give a "Think About the Earth" environmental fact; and Friday, we'd have a joke of the day.

But one day, while I was on the treadmill in the morning, the next song on the playlist was "Jump" by Van Halen. As I was running, I began to think, "There are few, if any, kids at my school who would even know what this song was, because it came out in 1984 . . ." It was a Wednesday morning, so Wednesdays became forever known as "We Dance Wednesdays." We always have a snippet of an upbeat song to dance to. Some are contemporary, some are older, but all have a lesson surrounding their genre, artist, meaning, etc. There is no better way to highlight different cultures than music, so highlighting African American, Latin X, Asian, etc. artists brings awareness to students in a meaningful and fun way.

As we continued to evolve, we created the following structure. Some consistent components are:

- Daily Birthdays

- Pledge of Allegiance

- Quote of the Week (usually tied into the monthly character theme or cultural/seasonal celebration)

- Character Theme

- Character Challenge each day (based upon the monthly theme)

- School-wide celebrations or reminders (e.g., bus expectations, cafeteria rules, etc.)

In addition to the consistent weekly items, there are daily highlights:

- **Mindfulness Monday:** A mindfulness mini-lesson (1–2 minutes) and breathing activity.

- **True Fact Tuesday:** A fun fact that is random or apropos based on the season, month, etc.

- **We Dance Wednesday:** A song and video to promote movement, dancing, fun, and cultural awareness, when possible.

- **Think About the Earth Thursday:** We alternate between sustainability ideas and children's books with themes that support our character theme or world culture. When we use books, I talk about the book, and a link is included for classrooms to view a read-aloud at another time during the day.

- **Joke Friday:** The most popular day of the week. We have 4–5 jokes that tend to be in the "dad joke" category but are made better (depending upon who you ask) by me explaining why they are funny—even if I don't need to. Students get into it, submit jokes by email or on post-its, and, without fail, stop me in the halls to comment on or talk about the day's jokes. We use seasonal themes when possible.

When the pandemic hit, the announcements were created and sent via video, using Touchcast, and emailed to all homes at the same time. This continued when we came back in A/B day cohorts. They became a huge symbol of consistency and solidarity in very difficult times. The unintended consequence was that it also included families in the daily operations of the school and shared the experience with them. I'd hear from grandparents who lived across the country, whose children or grandchildren shared the announcements with me each day.

We had a decision to make when we resumed a "normal" daily schedule. Using video became important, but the idea of a pre-recorded video just wasn't feasible (it took hours each night to arrange and record in Touchcast), so the compromise was to use Zoom and have classes watch live each day. The announcements were condensed a great deal in the Zoom version (I worked hard to keep them to five minutes or less, whereas the fully recorded announcements would run 10–12 minutes typically).

Through my "Principal's Cabinet," I had regular check-ins with staff to gauge what the best time and mechanism for sharing the announcements would be. We landed on a "live" version of the Zoom announcements to air at 8:45 a.m. (toward the beginning of the homeroom/morning meeting period), but that would also be recorded and emailed out, so that classes could watch at the end of the homeroom period or later if they had a special activity, such as band/orchestra, etc. That worked, but it kept me from tending to the post-arrival issues and check-ins. So now, I pre-record a Zoom with the same exact format and email just before arrival at 8:20 a.m., so that I'm available and present, but students and staff get a fresh, "almost live" version of the announcements.

Putting on This HAT: Start small. Maybe you have a great structure already in place for announcements, and you want to mix in fun by playing some music or mixing in jokes. Friday is a great day for jokes, to end the week on a light note. The most important thing is to start somewhere. The announcements can be a venue for you to be yourself and to model *having fun*. The great part is that there is no right or wrong way to do it, and you can change and evolve anytime you like. Just get started by adding one fun thing at a time into your normal routine!

Partnering with the Community's Seniors
Brian McCann

We graduate on the first Sunday in June at 1 p.m. The morning of each graduation event, I met my father when he was still alive at 7 a.m. mass in the church I grew up in to start the day off on a positive, reflective note, one that would help me partner with a higher power for no rain that afternoon.

When my dad passed, I continued this but looked at the congregation a little differently. I was one of the youngest in the church by far, and I did not know any of the adults who were present.

How could this be when I'm in the church I've attended since childhood in a community that I've worked in for the better part of three decades?

It seems that the community has grown older, and I had little connection to this demographic. There was an untapped partnership and an organic learning opportunity for my school.

I piloted two visits that year. The first would invite a cross-section of students to take a bus ride to the senior center and engage one-on-one with seniors in technology. We would bring the devices, front-load some senior-appropriate games to play, and then partake in some of their daily planned activities at the center.

The day was a big hit, with about 25 high-school students making new friends at our local senior center. After the tech games, high-school students joined the seniors in low-impact aerobics and many photographs. We learned of very different childhoods than our current students had: leaving school to work in the mills, supporting a family at an early age, and immigrating to a country where they did not speak the language.

This initial partnership was a great success. In turn, we invited seniors to take a school bus ride to the high school for a Valentine's Day lunch, followed by a performance by our theater students in the auditorium.

Many of the seniors had never ridden in a school bus before, since they were raised in urban areas where all children walked to school.

The fabulous cafeteria staff prepared a roast-turkey dinner for the Valentine's Day menu. Preschoolers from our childcare program made homemade cards.

It was indeed magic to watch two communities intersect on that day. The photos we took on those days reflect the joyful possibilities when two worlds make an effort to combine.

Having had a successful pilot, we returned the next year to implement Tech Help Desk to assist seniors at the center with everything from email to YouTube to Facebook.

The partnership could not continue when COVID began. Two subsequent school years were filled with ever-evolving restrictions on our social interactions, especially in school events. The chance for a field trip was non-existent at that point.

Putting on this HAT: They may not have ridden a school bus in more than 50, 60, or 70 years, but this group of community stakeholders was an important partnership. Actively engaging your community's senior citizens can only help build and strengthen a school culture. Partnerships like these also help the community prioritize its resources, so that they can see that education is not mutually exclusive for the young, but also for the young-at-heart.

CHAPTER 7

IMPACTFUL HATS

Reminding Students of Their *Why* on Day One
Brian McCann

I was blessed in my 18-year run as principal of the high school that I graduated from. I was able to see the school through a lot of change—I was part of five decennial accreditations of the school. I was part of the school's fabric for the bulk of six decades, from the 1970s to the present.

One of the most authentic actions that I regularly shared with my students was my actual high-school diploma that I had framed in my office. On the first day of the school year, I would take the diploma from my wall and bring it into the auditorium for the freshman class's first meeting.

I would ask them to take a moment before they went on to their first day of high school and take a look at this diploma. The diploma represents the culmination of the high-school experience, validation that you have succeeded in meeting requirements for many to go on to their next adventure.

The diploma had not changed in decades. By having students see an actual diploma from the high school that they were attending, they were able to visualize their end goal.

Despite the friends, the games, the plays, the concerts, the laughs, and the tears, a diploma is still the common objective for all who attend high school.

My favorite years were the ones when I gathered a few unknowing freshmen in the first minutes of their secondary career and took a picture with them and my diploma. Fast-forward four years: I would recreate this same shot on the day they graduated from high school.

Putting on this HAT: Don't underestimate the power of visuals. Students would routinely comment on my diploma if they would visit me in my office. The ability to capture these moments of a plan and its subsequent fulfillment is priceless.

Some students plod from one day to the next without a goal or focus. The visualization of a journey's endgame recalibrates and gives the next four years deeper meaning.

It's more than a piece of paper: a diploma is a ticket to tomorrow, even if you never seemed to have left high school, like me.

Do More Than Expected
Andrew Marotta

You'll never go wrong doing more than expected. Yes, there are requirements, union obligations, and a lot of "musts" throughout the school year, yet it is the simple *just doing a little more than expected* that so many people will remember.

Think about the last time you went to a restaurant. If you received a special seat, maybe a dessert to share on the house, or something a little extra, it was very much appreciated. What about at a hotel? Something extra, a room upgrade, even the smallest gesture, is always well received by the guest.

These types of acts in schools can change lives. They can inspire the young minds and hearts of kids as well as enthuse those on the front lines teaching and supporting our kids.

What are some examples of what we are talking about? Let's start with recognition. Everyone likes to be recognized for their efforts, and, as our moms taught us, it's not what you say, it's how you say it. Well, in this case, it is not what the recognition is, but how you do it.

The teacher or student wins an award. Regular: You call the kid or teacher down and hand them the certificate on regular black-and-white paper with a photocopied signature on it. Maybe you say their name over the loudspeaker.

Doing more than expected:

- Get the heavy-duty card stock paper (yes, the kind that jams the printer!), get the certificate printed in ink with real, live signatures, maybe even of the students in the class or team teachers.

- Don't just give the certificate—write a short note explaining why the kid/teacher won the award.

- Take a picture, and post it on social media with an authentic message.

- Mail a letter home recognizing the event, and send a real copy of the picture of you handing the award to the person.

- I have even started autographing the picture to the person with #s like "#awesome," "#youareamzaing." They'll hang that up in their space at home and remember the moment for a long time.

- Publicly recognize achievements at assemblies, board meetings, and cafe spaces.

- Pins, lanyards, and points of pride that the person can display to share the good news.

Putting on this HAT: Yes, I understand that you can't do everything on this list all the time for everyone. It is just not possible. You can, though, do it more often than not. *Andrew, I'm already swamped with so much bad stuff, discipline referrals, and angry parents. I don't have time for fluffy stuff.*

Which came first? The chicken or the egg? How do you change the culture? How do you swing your pendulum of work from bad to good? Negative to positive? Start doing these things with some extra spice and soul, and they become contagious. You start to feel better, and you enrich and excite those around you with good vibes. Busy? Delegate a lot of this to others, and spread the joy.

In the end, you are making a memorable moment of joy for someone you work with or a student you serve. Make it the best it can be! #domorethanexpected

JumpStart
Jay Billy

For many years, we've tried to find ways to help students adjust to school. For those of us who work in early-childhood education, the first couple weeks of school are all about teaching school behaviors, building relationships, and getting students comfortable in their new setting. When students arrive for kindergarten, they come with a variety of experiences. No matter where you work, you'll have students who have always been in daycare and preschool. You'll have students who recently began leaving the home for a partial-day daycare/preschool experience, and you'll have students who have no experience in school or group-play/learning settings. This can lead to a lot of anxiety for students and their families.

One idea that I was able to implement years ago using Title I funds (it is now a budgeted item) was to do what we call a JumpStart program, where incoming kindergarten students who may not have had any preschool experiences are invited in for a couple of hours a day for a few weeks in the summer to help them in their adjustment and make them more comfortable to the transition when the school year starts.

Our district is very diverse and has students who come from all over the world. Some families don't have the means to send their children to preschool: Some don't want to, and some don't believe in it. We also have a large number of students who don't speak English in the home (second-language students.) We started this program years ago with just our Title I schools, and the kindergarten students were identified because they had no preschool experience. They were the ones we invited in originally. We used Title I money to pay teachers and tried to get our English as a Second Language educators to join in as well to support the new students. We started small. Our teachers, who were all early-childhood teachers, were able to provide the students with early learning experiences and teach them school behaviors.

Although each school is different and every transition is different, kindergarten is always the big step for families and kids. During our JumpStart program, we make sure that students get past their early jitters and feel as comfortable as possible. Some of the things we do are:

- Independent play

- Teach them to line up and get teacher's attention appropriately

- Teach them to sit and listen to stories

- Work on taking turns

- Teach and observe basic skills such as pencil grip, scissors, cutting, writing, coloring

- Practice eating in the cafeteria

- Practice playing on the playground and learning safety rules

- Work on solving conflict

- Fire drills, emergency drills

- Do basic assessments

- Practice sitting on and riding a bus, and learning bus rules

- Get accustomed to finding your way around the building and learning where the different special classes are located

Putting on this HAT: Whenever we can give our kids an early opportunity for learning routines, feeling comfortable, and understanding expectations, we should try. JumpStart was created for our early learners (kindergarten), but we have found that students who transition from building to building benefit from exposure to this type of transitional experience. Especially after COVID, we opened JumpStart up to multiple grades because students hadn't been in the buildings for a while or hadn't been used to being near other students. We now do JumpStart for our fourth graders, who move on to another building. When they transition to middle school or high school, there is a full orientation day, where students get to know more about the school, learn how to get around, and how to be part of the system that is school. As students get older, it's great to see student leaders leading these sessions and tours of the building. It shows that their voices are heard and that students are what makes a school.

opPORTunities
Andrew Marotta

I love this. Someone in my district put this on a bulletin board, and I fell in love with it. My school district is Port Jervis, New York, and we create opportunities for staff, students, and teachers. How can we make this a priority in our schools? Let's start with students:

Clubs, activities, sports, new sports, intramurals, student-led activities, and more—so many new opPORTunities out there for students. Let's use the example of flag football, e-sports, and vex-robotics. These are newer ideas, sports, and activities for kids that are taking off not only in Port Jervis, New York, but in many schools. What is the culture in your school to get an opPORTunity started? Can people freely propose an idea, get it weighed in on, and then, boom, it can be on its way? Or are there all kinds of red tape, negotiations, approvals, and more?

What about the adults, teachers, and staff? Are there opPOR-Tunities for leadership, growth, freedoms, and more? And how do you promote this in your schools? Teacher- and staff-led activities can be some of the strongest and most effective, because they are not top-down. They are from colleague to colleague, staff to staff. What do staff-development days look like? Can staff present? Can staff pilot different products, programs, tools, and more?

Putting on this HAT: One great way to hear, see, and promote opPORTunities is the activity: *I wish we had,* or *I wish we could.* At a staff meeting, professional-development day, student-group meeting, etc., hang up big post-it notes asking the prompting questions: *I wish we had,* or *I wish we could,* or *My idea is . . .* Then, let it fly. See what comes of it. It doesn't mean you are agreeing to all of it or can do it, either. You are just allowing the process of expression, exploration, and possible future opPORTunities for your people. Listen to what they have to say, and see what you can do. **Allowing the voice and process is a HAT within itself.**

The Red Bicycle
Andrew Marotta

In the summer of 2021, I visited the Muhammad Ali Center in Louisville, Kentucky. I was always intrigued by Muhammad Ali and his large, loud persona. "I'm the greatest," he would yell, and I was hooked. *"Float like a butterfly, sting like a bee."* I wanted to be energetic, confident, and great.

I learned so much about Ali that day, including the red-bicycle story. How did he get started in boxing? When and where did he begin?

It all started with his red bike being stolen off the streets of Louisville. Ali, or, back then, he was Cassius Clay, was fuming. "I'm gonna knock him out. I'm going to hit him!" Clay yelled until a police officer who was working in the area came into contact with Ali. He tried to calm him down and told him, "Listen, son, you go hit that guy who stole your bike, you're gonna get yourself in trouble. You have the right to be angry. Come to my gym after school today, and you can take out your frustrations on the bag. Hit away." Cassius Clay did just that. He did go to the gym that day—he was angry, and he did pound away at the punching bag. The rest is history.

Putting on this HAT: What is your gym? Where is your hook for a kid or staff member who might be struggling? How can you redirect some behaviors that maybe are negative and turn them into positive ones? Absorb this story of the power of a single moment, a single interaction.

They happen in schools all day long. How can you recognize them? Capitalize on them? Make your impact felt? Did that police officer way back then know at the time what his impact would be by the actions he took? No way . . . and neither will you, in the moment. Look for the red bicycle moments, and put your gifts and talents into action.

Secret Society of Readers
Jay Billy

We want to celebrate literacy in all forms, especially in our elementary schools. Often, the day gets filled with programs and curriculum, and we forget the importance of building and sustaining the love of reading. When we teach students to read, we open up the world for them and give them opportunities that they would not have otherwise. Reading takes them to places they may never physically get to travel to and teaches them things about cultures and societies that they won't learn in class.

In *Kids Deserve It!* Todd Nesloney and Adam Welcome introduce an idea called the "Secret Society of Readers," which I was able to make happen at our school. You know—those kids who come off of the bus reading books and don't put them down, even when they are walking? You know—those kids who, given the choice and opportunity, would just be reading books all day? One of my children is one of these types of readers. Since she was young, she went everywhere with a book. She loves all types of books, but what hooked her were fantasy books and books delving into Greek mythology. She is now in law school, but whenever she has time, she has five or more books checked out of the local library. She is the kind of person who waits for the next book in a series and, right before it comes out, she reads all of the preceding books again. You know those kids.

For kids like my daughter—or simply to promote this type of literacy growth—we created the "Secret Society of Readers." I reach out to my third grade teachers and ask for them to identify those kids who, given the choice, would be knee-deep in a book rather than play or goof off. I put the list together, and then I arrange a time with our librarian for them to visit.

I set up a meeting with each student individually and tell them that they are being invited to join the "Secret Society of Readers." It is so secret that they can't tell their friends (but they may tell their parents). We will all meet in the library on Fridays during the morning meeting time. I explain that I will tell their teachers and that they can just leave the classroom without explanation to their peers. We make it mysterious but must continue to keep it a secret.

On the first day of the meeting, they come down to the library, and I reiterate that all they have to do is keep this a secret, and we will continue to do this on a weekly basis. Basically, I'm giving them the gift of time to just sit and read. They can go into a corner, sit at a table, lie on the floor, anything they want. They get a one-half hour of uninterrupted time to read. When they return to class, they can't tell anyone where they have been or what they have been doing. This is a gift to these kinds of kids, and they get how important secrecy is.

The students just love this, and it is something that is *just for them*. They appreciate the fact that we noticed their love of reading, and it gives me the chance to get to know them as readers, too. They become very protective of this group and this time. Obviously, this is voluntary, and, sometimes, they may choose to stay in class because there is something fun going on that they don't want to miss. Most of the time, they are sneaking in to ask me, "When is the next time that SSOR is meeting?" Usually, after a few months, I will sit with the students and ask them if they have any friends they think would be a good fit for the SSOR. They are usually very protective of this group, so they really think hard before making recommendations.

At the end of the year, we disclose to the rest of the classes where the students have been going each week. This gives others a reason to see the importance of reading and the benefits that can be derived from the time spent.

Putting on this HAT: Whenever you can make a group of kids who are passionate about something feel important and recognize the power of their passions, you are building them up for a lifetime of growth and encouraging them to continue to do something that we know will make them better. The secrecy of this "special group" is a key component of making the "Secret Society of Readers" special. You could do this with any subject or specific activity where you have a group of kids who have a common interest. Think about giving kids who are interested in gaming or programming time to just play or program. Think about your STEM kids who just love to build, and you want to find time to enjoy and build on that passion. This may be the one thing that kids look forward to on a weekly basis and keeps them coming back. It may be the one thing that they remember from their time in your school or classroom.

Community Love
Michael Brown

Michael C. Brown has been a highly regarded Maryland educator for 21 years. Principal Michael C. Brown has distinguished himself as a transformational school leader and equity pioneer within Carroll County Public Schools (CCPS). As a Principal in CCPS, in 2019, Michael was awarded the ETM (Education That is Multicultural) Principal of the Year for his work centered around diversity and equity. Michael is also the President-Elect for the MASSP (Maryland Association of Secondary School Principals).

Every school year has its difficulties. As school leaders, we are bound to a specific, systemic academic cycle that rotates but rarely changes. Within that cycle of routines, structures, and protocols, there can be moments of spontaneity as well as moments of amazement and wonder that can bring any person sheer joy.

On a seemingly regular night in early September 2022, our school would be met with an unprecedented situation that showed us that fear, hope, and love are real action words and that those emotions can happen in an instant.

Greyson Lyons, a junior lineman for Winters Mill High School, with one minute, 53 seconds left in the second quarter of a season-opening game against host St. John's Catholic Prep, collapsed and did not get up. After what seemed like a normal high-school football play, Greyson wobbled and fell without notice or warning.

Athletic trainers, coaches, and even some medical people from the crowd all converged on the scene to assist. Mouth-to-mouth resuscitation, chest compressions, and a defibrillator were all performed on him to revive his heart and get him breathing again.

At the time, I was at home and recall receiving a call from our career coordinator, Bobbi Hollingsworth. She was crying and appeared to be in a frantic state as I tried desperately to make out what she was saying. "Greyson is down, and I don't think he is breathing!" As I tried to calm her down, I realized at that moment what exactly was happening and how desperate the situation was. *This kid may not make it if somebody there doesn't act quickly and with precision.*

Back at the game, both teams were kneeling on their respective sidelines, and there was not a dry eye to be found.

It was at that moment that something amazing started to happen: Individuals from St. John's Catholic Prep School started to pray and hope that this young man would recover and live.

Once the medical persons from the field gave the signal that Greyson had been revived, a huge cheer broke out all over the crowd. What proceeded from then on was also a miracle. Greyson had to be airlifted by the Maryland State Police Trooper 3 helicopter so he could be taken to Shock Trauma. In the process of taking him to Shock Trauma, Greyson would flatline again and had to be revived by the medical personnel on the helicopter. In a very short period of time, Greyson was able to make a full recovery, which was an absolute blessing.

The following week, Greyson was able to lead the Falcon football team out onto the field at the start of the next game. The sheer joy on the faces of every person in the stadium was indescribable. His father, a Deputy Police Officer for Carroll County, gave me the biggest hug and looked into my eyes like only a relieved father would, and thanked me. I felt I hadn't done anything but support the student and his family and assured them that the school was doing everything we could for Greyson in order for him to feel comfortable once he returned to school later that week.

The outpouring of support didn't stop that night, either. His GoFundMe account soared to more $34,000, with people from all over the state—and beyond—giving to help offset expensive medical bills from when he was in the hospital. Students, staff, and community members from the St. John's Catholic Prep School also continued to show their support for Greyson. They planned to wear all gray—as a school—at their next home game to show their love and solidarity for him and the school.

Greyson's home school, Winters Mill High School, bought bracelets with the phrase, "Greyson Lyon Strong" to help him with financial support, as the proceeds also went to help with any costly bills from that problematic night. Lastly, schools all across Carroll County also wore gray and bought bracelets in support of Greyson and the family.

Putting on this HAT: All of this love and support for a person whom many had never met. They didn't know him, but it shows what can happen through the power of emotion and where that wave can take you. All stakeholders in this situation become leaders, modeling empathy, compassion, and the power of community.

Hey, Just Checking In
Andrew Marotta

I like the Friday afternoon text or call. Not too late that people have started their weekend, dinner, etc. Maybe 3–4 p.m., maybe 4:30 p.m. A quick text or call: Hey—how are you? Hope you had a good week. Thank you for your amazing efforts this week at school. I wanted to compliment you on an amazing _____(fill in the blank—concert, lesson, performance, phone call, meeting, presentation, and so on). This is a simple way to give positive recognition quickly while ending the workweek for members of your staff as well as you. Not only do you make the other person feel good about leaving work and something they did, you make yourself feel good by completing this HAT.

Putting on this HAT: Please don't confuse this with a good old-fashioned. in-person, look-in-the-eye compliment. Talking and connecting with others is always best. Yet on a busy Friday, as you are heading to dinner with your family or leaving for the weekend, spend five minutes in your car, with the windows rolled down, breathing deeply, and send four or five texts to staff. Send several messages through your school system to students. Reach those in your circles who deserve a positive message or need the positive message. Both are very important. I believe these small deposits in the lives of those we serve go a long way in building relationships with our people. No matter your title, no matter your role, the impact can be felt immediately with this HAT.

Quiet Moment
Brian McCann

Sammi was new to my school in her junior year. I did not know a lot about her except that I would say, "Good Morning," when I saw her or notice that she had a new boyfriend as the year went on.

Sammi appeared quiet, yet content. She always smiled. I noticed that she had made a connection with a young art teacher who encouraged her each day. Despite some minor attendance issues, she was well-acclimated to school and high school life.

I had no idea.

It wasn't until I brought up Sammi by chance to the art teacher that I learned her backstory: she was the only child of a single mom who had Stage 4 cancer. Doctors said her mom's passing was imminent.

The art teacher mentioned that Sammi would like to speak with me. We met soon after, and she revealed to me that there was a possibility that she might be missing some school in the next few weeks. She wanted me to know this in advance so that I wouldn't think ill of her or that she didn't care about school.

I confided that I was aware of her mom's situation and fully understood and supported her any time that the daughter would be with her. I told her to let me worry about any unexcused absences from school as well as communicate with her teachers.

In essence, I gave Sammi permission to begin closure with her mom. Since school was one of the few stable environments in her life at present, Sammi now felt she could be both a good daughter and good student.

Close to the end of the school year, Sammi's mom passed over the weekend. The art teacher texted me on Sunday, and I was prepared on Monday to begin grieving with her.

To my surprise, Sammi came to school. Again, it was a place of stability and consistency. I purposely spent time in the art room that morning when Sammi was scheduled to have class. I acknowledged her loss and just sat with her.

Six months later, my wife was in a conversation with another art teacher from the high school. She mentioned that Sammi was asking for me after I retired and reminded the teacher that, despite all I had to do in the school day, I chose to spend a few quiet moments in a classroom filled with students just after her mom passed.

And how much this gesture meant to her.

And, in turn, to me.

Putting on this HAT: Grieving is tricky and different at all school levels. After an initial acknowledgment, sometimes quiet is best. Without making prior connections with this student, my words or actions might not have had any meaning, or even been welcomed. Every moment of the school day counts.

Choosing Traditions Over Nostalgia
Jeanne Muzi

Jeanne Muzi is the proud principal of Slackwood Elementary School in Lawrence Township, New Jersey. She has a passion for cultivating curiosity, for questioning, and for finding creative approaches to problem-solving. Jeanne is always a teacher at heart and was named the 2008–2009 New Jersey State Teacher of the Year.

Every school cultivates its own climate and culture while establishing what is valued, focused on, and celebrated within its learning community. Eventually, every school creates meaningful traditions, but some also cling to school-centric nostalgia. Tradition and nostalgia both look to the past to impact the future, but traditions are positive and meaningful, and exude gratitude for what has helped to make a school special. In contrast, nostalgia is a wistfulness for the past and often a reaching back to "the good old days." Tradition connects to pride and brings strength to a forward-looking vision.

Nostalgia yearns for the past and the ways things have always been done. One of the most heartfelt acts that can be shared with teachers and students is to embrace meaningful and positive traditions that build community and connections while eschewing nostalgic practices that keep students bound to the past.

We all have traditions that shape the school year, from the ways we welcome new students and staff to the final Clap-Outs when we say farewell to students who are moving on. It is essential to embrace the traditions that build a strong culture and say goodbye to things that don't. Taking time to reflect on the books being shared, the projects students are working on, and the voices we include helps to develop inclusive and celebratory traditions, which can, and should, evolve. As we change how the day and year ebb and flow through traditions, our students, their families, and our colleagues experience greater joy in learning, and feel they are a part of something special! It might be something as small as moving a pen-and-paper task to become a digital task or including a virtual component to meetings and events. We might look to alter a space, take down outdated artwork, eliminate a fundraiser, or throw out a schedule if they no longer support a forward-looking vision. Need a few more quick ideas? Here are a few places to start:

Kicking off a school year: Reflect on the Getting to Know You activities and the Ice-Breakers you use each year. Consider things like "Find Someone Who" and "Bring in Something from Your Summer," which are used year after year on opening days to introduce students to each other. These activities can become redundant and can spotlight inequities. Creating fresh traditions can focus on creativity, collaboration, and communication, and enable all students to be a valued part of the "Getting to Know You" work. For example, before NASA launches any mission, the astronauts work together to create a patch which combines words, symbols, and images to communicate the vision and goals of the mission. A patch design can capture the mission of a new school year and help build community in a new class. Once a teacher has introduced the students to NASA Mission Patches, the designing can begin. A whole-class patch can be designed collaboratively, small groups can create their own patches, or each student can hand-sketch or use a drawing app to create their own individual patches. These patches can be displayed throughout the year, reproduced on class materials like newsletters, anthologies, and slide shows, and shared with families. The patch designs can also be changed and updated as the year goes on. Another creative new tradition can be designing a logo for the start of the new year. Students at every level recognize logos from websites, video games, superheroes, and so on. Challenging students to work together (or individually) to design a logo that represents their identity, hopes, and dreams communicates the importance of creativity and establishes the cornerstone that, in their new classroom, throughout the school year, they will be creators, designers, and thinkers. Year after year, new logos can be added to student portfolios, thus opening up a new tradition. Logo design is also very engaging and an effective introduction activity for Teacher-Induction events or as a part of Professional Development.

Wrapping up an amazing school year: A wonderful tradition that can be started at any age is the "Letter to my Future Self," which has students writing their hopes, dreams, favorite activities, and unique aspects of their life to their future selves as they graduate from high school. Having the graduating seniors return to their elementary schools to read the letters written years ago is a wonderful way of connecting the past to the future. The letter often provides a lesson in resilience and goal setting. Having high school seniors visit with younger students is also a meaningful tradition, since it gives the older students a chance to say, "I have sat where you are sitting. I did it, and so will you." Opening the younger students' eyes to all the possibilities the future offers is time well spent and provides opportunities for mentorship and connection. Student-created memory books and videos also provide another unique way to capture a year and reflect on everything the students experienced during a special block of time in their lives. Having students create these items puts them at the center of the projects. They are writers, designers, directors, and publishers. Creative traditions provide time for students to look back and look forward as they continue their educational journey.

Putting on this HAT: As we look at those things that have always been a part of our school and community, we must remember to think about what is adding to us and who we want to be. The "That's the way we've always done it" mindset is no longer a useful tool for making our schools better. Be reflective of the choices you are making for your students and their families; take the opportunity to take an inventory of the nostalgic practices that are in place, and think about ways to replace them without forgetting the past traditions.

The Second Chance
Andrew Marotta

School life can be challenging sometimes. Lots of regulations, expectations, and a fast-moving train of bells, periods, and deadlines.

Throw in rough weather, state testing, and teenagers, and it can be one tough mix.

I believe in the power of second chances. Giving people a break when something was not up to par or not done right. I've heard all the jargon: enforce the rules, be tough, hold people accountable, students need to learn the hard lessons, etc., etc. But really, what are those lessons? Deadlines or short leashes? Or are we here to change lives and make memorable moments for kids and staff?

What is more memorable for you: when the cop, emotionless, hands you a speeding ticket, or when he/she gives you a break and tells you they expect to see you at the next volunteer event, helping out the community?

We all have choices working and leading in schools. Yes, we have to follow procedures, and we want to be consistent, but let's think about people's lives—and how much they need compassion, understanding, and some TLC in the moment of a troubled situation. If the person (teacher, student, staff, or parent) is of bad character, they will do it again, and then, you enforce the rules, but let's give each other second chances. Life is short, and people deserve a break when they are done.

Putting on this HAT: Here are two examples of second chances that I am proud of because of the way they were handled—unconventionally yet impactfully:

First example: Student speeding on campus: Easy fix—take away his driving privileges for 30 days. Bam! Enforce the rule, and show strength, right? I heard the kid out: he begged for forgiveness. He offered to volunteer, make amends, and promised it would not happen again. Second chance? Why or why not?

The student received the following:

- a discipline referral

- only could drive his siblings to school for the next 30 days

- had to park in the secondary parking lot

- had to do three volunteer events—positively volunteering—at the school

- lastly, he had to speak to the next group of young drivers coming up as part of a safety seminar.

His parents were in full agreement and grateful for the impact this event had on their son. Did I get criticized for not giving the hard consequence? Yes, I did, but what was best at that moment? What was most impactful for the student? I believe we chose the right HAT for this scenario.

Second situation: Teacher says something inappropriate to a student. The teacher had an excellent track record of being a good person, yet in that moment of a heated exchange with a disrespectful student, she slipped and said something inappropriate. Should she have been "written up"? Absolutely. Did she deserve a second chance? Most definitely, and she did, indeed, get one.

I'm a fan of the letter "me to you" and not placing the letter about the incident in their permanent work file. Was the person remorseful? Did they own their actions and make good on it? All of these are factors in those decisions.

The teacher apologized to the student, called the parents, told them what had occurred, and was truly sorry for what they said.

They got a "letter me to you" acknowledging the occurrence and encouraging it to not happen again. They were grateful to me for a second chance and felt empowered by the way that they handled it. Is this holding people accountable for their actions without the iron fist of enforcing the rules? I believe so. When the conditions are right, give this HAT a try.

CHAPTER 8

HATS BRIMMING WITH POSITIVITY

The Power of Inclusivity
Brian McCann

In her senior year at my high school, Anna F. was selected Homecoming Queen by her peers.

It was a joyous night in the high school, with teenagers dressed up in a wide fashion range of evening attire. At least three-quarters of the school's student population was present on this Friday night, and the music was rocking from the gymnasium.

But the highlight of the evening was when the Homecoming King and Queen were announced. This year, a first-string football player was chosen as the Homecoming King, and the crowd went wild when the Queen was announced as the student he would be escorting this evening.

Anna.

Not many students had classes with Anna, although she was a presence in the building. Anna was a student in an alternative classroom that spent most of the day in a substantially separate setting.

You might see her in the cafeteria at lunch or in the gymnasium during a phys-ed class, but most students at this high school did not have a core academic or elective class with Anna.

Anna was a high school student with Down syndrome.

In order for students in Anna's program to attend the Homecoming Dance, provisions had to be made in advance for special coverage so that an identified adult would help supervise and facilitate the evening without hovering over a handful of students during the evening.

Even though some special arrangements were in place, Anna entered the school for this dance check-in in the same manner as every other student. She stood in the long line and waited patiently. She was Breathalyzed as all other students were, and she followed the pathway created for this dance in the gym, as others did.

Senior students were polled for the event as to who they wanted as their Homecoming King and Queen and their Court. The announcement by the building principal of the results was the high point of the evening, the moment curated with the Yearbook photographer and almost simultaneously on various social-media platforms.

Although many schools across the country have given up traditions like homecoming and prom kings and queens, the students at my high school have used both of these special annual events to celebrate many of their peers who have successfully navigated high school in conjunction with being a teenager with an identified disability.

Hats off to the students who recognize the importance of inclusivity and seizing the opportunities to celebrate their peers who may have been only in the shadows in the past. These simple-yet-profound actions are reflective of an adult community that model the importance of honing and maintaining an inclusive culture. The purposeful intentions of adults directly influence the actions of the students, thereby creating a culture where all are truly welcomed, acknowledged, celebrated, and a vibrant part of the school's fabric.

Hats off to the adults who use their influential superpowers for the benefit of the entire student body.

Putting on this HAT: Anna's coupling with the Homecoming King center court on the gym floor might have been the briefest dance of the evening, but it represented the fruits of a community's insistence that all students truly means *all* students in this town.

Signage: Positive or Negative?
Andrew Marotta

Do this. Go there. Sit here. Be quiet. You are not allowed to do this ____. You must follow these rules. Do not, do not, do not, etc., etc. Soooo many rules in schools. Look around your school. What does the signage look like in your school? How are the signs worded? Do they tell the students all the things they are not supposed to do, or do they model positivity? What are the expectations and ways students/staff can complete these actions?

I challenge you to take a look at all the signs around your district. Count them, chart them, and review the verbiage. Are they written in a negative manner? *Do not, no*, etc., or are they written in a positive light?

One of the biggest campaigns we had in Port Jervis Schools was getting rid of smoking in the schools. It was a terrible situation, and our halls and bathrooms were filled with smoke, nonstop. Through the power of collaboration and perseverance, we launched the "Proud to be Smoke-Free" campaign. Were we smoke-free at the time of the signage/campaign? *No!* Not at all. Did this help with our communication and expectation of everyone? *Absolutely!* Many of our signs had the main message of "Proud to be Smoke-Free," "Thank You for Not Smoking," and "Make Good Choices. Stay Smoke-Free!"

This successful group effort of being smoke-free is one that I was most proud to be a part of.

Putting on this HAT: These were two signs I put up during the crazy days of the Tik Tok challenges where kids were destroying their schools for no reason. Ripping down dispensers, breaking toilets, damaging toilet-paper holders, and more. *It was a rough time.*

If I yelled at the boys, put up strongly worded signs, or other scare tactics, would those have worked? I'll never know, and my mindset through this all was to "stay positive." *We will get through this.*

These signs worked. One got ripped down, and I replaced it immediately. I was intentional in really taping down all the sides heavily, so someone had to work really hard to rip it off. I felt these signs were:

- 🎩 Written respectfully, and in turn, produced respect.

- 🎩 Modeled the behavior we were looking for saying "Please" and "Thank you."

- 🎩 Inspiring one to pause and think about what they were doing.

- 🎩 Asking students to be leaders and builders.

On your journey, try this exercise of looking at your signage, and see what you come up with!

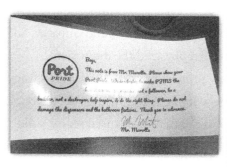

The Kindness Bus
Jay Billy

Character, empathy, and kindness are some of the most important things that we try to teach in our schools. We continually talk about being kind to our friends and those around us. Sure, we focus on academics and work to give our students the skills they will need in the future, but our mission is to build better humans. One way we do this is by continually emphasizing the importance of being kind and modeling what kindness looks like for all around us.

Although this seems like it's a no-brainer for an elementary school, not everyone believes that schools are the place for students to focus their kindness superpowers. When I first came to my present school, there were many great teachers who focused on character as well as academics, but a real outward focus on kindness wasn't as pronounced. People knew that I felt it was important to have our kids understand the importance of kindness and empathy, but some may have thought I over-emphasized the discussion.

It is common, when a new principal starts, that families want to make sure you know them or find out a little more about you. I once met with a parent who was extremely focused on his child's academic success and the rigor of our programs. This parent believed that all of the focus on character was wasted time for academics. He even said to me one day, "Kindness isn't going to get my kid into Princeton." There really is no comeback to that except to continue to assure families that we are doing our best to give children the skills necessary not only to be successful in life but also to become good human beings. It is important that our kids understand that we need to take care of each other and those in our world who need help.

Throughout the year, elementary schools do a number of things that show the importance of teaching and living in a world of kindness. There are many external opportunities such as the "Great Kindness Challenge," which is an international event over one week, where students check off activities of kindness. During World Kindness Day, students and people around the world commit to acts of kindness in order to make our world a better place.

In our school, all of our teachers understand the importance and focus on being kind. However, I have one teacher who has taken it to the next level. Mrs. Krisak is a kindergarten teacher who loves what she does and loves the children she works with. It is evident in everything that she does that she was born to teach kindergarten. She also takes kindness to the next level. Her students all make shirts that speak of kindness and wear them on special occasions. Whenever you walk into her classroom, you can feel the warmth and love coming from the children, and she gives it right back.

A couple of years ago, Mrs. Krisak's classroom had made "Kindness Posters" that they wanted to take around town and put in local businesses and public places. Mrs. Krisak figured she'd just deliver them after work one day and spread the love through our community. She knew it would be more impactful if she could figure a way to have the kids deliver them, but it's not so easy or equitable to try to do it after school, so she came to me and our assistant superintendent and asked about getting a bus to do the deliveries during the school day. You'd think this would be an easy thing, but not necessarily because of the cost of drivers and the availability of buses. Of course, I said, "Yes, but let's see if we can make it happen." Our assistant superintendent also gave the go-ahead and reached out to our transportation department. Before you knew it, we had scheduled the bus trip.

The day for the trip came, and all of Mrs. Krisak's kindergarteners had their kindness shirts on and their posters ready. They boarded the bus and went from business to business, dropping off posters and asking the proprietors to put them up. They went to the local bakery, deli, diners, Dunkin' Donuts, Quickie Marts, and even to the police station and town hall. All of these places welcomed our kids, were gracious in putting up their signs, and took time to speak to our kids and thank them for their kindness and their love. When the students returned, they were so filled with joy and excitement. For many, it was more than just passing out signs—it gave them such a feeling of accomplishment by sharing their kindness and joy with others and seeing the local businesses share it right back.

Since that first trip on the "Kindness Bus," Mrs. Krisak's Kindness Kids have become somewhat legendary within our little community. Whenever I stop at the diner or the Dunkin' Donuts and see their signs, I know that they have made our community a better place to live in and our world a kinder place. When people see their signs, it puts a smile on their faces and reminds them to be kind.

You can see Krisak's Kindness Kids and the Kindness Bus here:

https://bit.ly/HATSKindnessBus

Putting on this HAT: Kindness isn't just for elementary-school kids. We must continue to remind our students about the importance of empathy and kindness. One of the most equitable things we can do is to share our kindness with the community. When our families know and understand that our schools are teaching more than just academics, they will begin to share the values and participate in the acts of kindness that they see their children sharing. It makes our world a better place for everyone.

And We're Back
Brian McCann

The return to school after our pandemic hiatus was fraught with many changes and journeys down school roads that were previously uncharted. Schools were left to figure things out by themselves, oftentimes reacting to a state mandate that had been changed or updated on a Friday afternoon for Monday implementation.

Like many, we were doing the best we could. We returned with masks, with a diminished population each day. Assigned seats at all times, staggered passing times, and one-way hallways. Single-table seating in the cafeteria, all facing toward the kitchen; restrictions in many areas of the school.

And no snow days.

The superintendent deemed that since we were now pro-grammed for online learning, especially for the students who were learning at home that specific day, there would be no need for a snow day.

Inclement weather would be met with business as usual, with teachers facilitating from home and students expected to be present and on time in each class for that day.

For me, no snow days also meant no snow-day videos. More about these in Chapter 9.

After the success of the past three years, this was saddening to me. What had transformed into a community's expectations had been taken away from us. Sure, I understood the rationale behind the decision, but I was still a little miffed that our momentum in our school community for an annual video had now been thwarted.

We had a couple of snowstorms that affected the school day that year. And we conducted business "sort of as usual" through virtual platforms. It wasn't really fun or especially fruitful, but these days did count as a school day in our state calendar.

A little more than a year after school closed, state officials gave the go-ahead to return to school full-time in April 2021. There was great excitement in coming back to school with the two largest cohorts of students together.

And this gave me an idea. Can we celebrate through song that we are back?

I assembled my snow-day team, penciled a parody song inspired by the Broadway phenomenon *Hamilton*, and watched the theater and video teacher start to work on a project that might have been the first semblance of something "normal' that year.

The video teacher assembled his more-seasoned senior-class veterans and storyboarded a simple journey through the school that celebrated the return, the changes, and the precautions that were taking place.

I even shared the stage with my assistant principal. Well, maybe not *shared*, but he was in multiple shots.

The theater teacher found tracks and helped me record the audio tracks.

We took great pains to ensure and publicize that the filming of this public service announcement was in accord with all state and local guidelines.

And then we dropped the video on the day that students returned to school. Here's a link to the video:

https://bit.ly/HATSAndwereback

The response was wild. We were literally picked up by every Providence and Boston television station that day. Crews came down, and additional interviews were conducted digitally. There was tremendous excitement from not only our school community but also from the area as a whole.

I even got a call that someone heard my singing on a radio station in central Massachusetts.

News stations don't want to present only negative news. It seems you see schools on the news only when test scores have fallen, violence has occurred, or a sports team captured a state title.

The everyday joy of school is an underrepresented news story idea.

We just made it easy for stations to report on us. We kept it lively, topical, and short, so that they could play most of the clip in less than 90 seconds.

Print media loved the story as well. This appeared on the local paper's front page during that week:

https://bit.ly/HATSHamiltonarticle

Putting on this HAT: Schools should make it easy for the local media to celebrate your school. Develop relationships with a reporter at EACH local news outlet. Don't be afraid to share your story with a larger television market. As this return-to-school story reflects, news agencies do enjoy sharing a *positive* story about your school. It was the team effort of administrators, teachers, and students who reunited under very extreme circumstances to put together a fun, inspiring, and hopeful video.

In the long run, we didn't need a snow day to celebrate our ongoing risk-taking. We just needed each other.

Oooh, Yeah!!!!
Andrew Marotta

I love slogans, creative commercial jingles, and rally cries for teams and organizations. Think of your favorite commercial jingle. You can visualize the person saying it—right? I think that the ability to visualize a commercial or jingle says a lot about branding as well as the message of the company or person themselves.

I have been blessed and fortunate to work with so many great people over the years in Port Jervis, New York. It is a wonderful school community, filled with passionate and talented educators and wonderful families. In my opinion, it's the definition of a true proud community.

I recently noticed one particular employee, Donald Burke. He shows up each day with great enthusiasm using the phrase loudly and boldly **"Oooh, yeah"** very often. When he would greet me in the morning, he would offer a warm and welcoming greeting of "Good morning, Oooh yeah." Midday, I would ask "How's it going?" and he would respond with "Oooh, yeah." So many varying situations, and they would either start or end with "Oooh, yeah," a smile, and a laugh.

At first, I thought that it was different, and after a while, it started to catch on. I started responding with "Oooh, yeah" and maybe a fist bump. Then an "Oooh, yeah" and a high-five. It felt contagious and was actually quite uplifting. I felt more energized and more enthusiastic after hearing it and saying it. He started to say it louder and more often. It was really starting to catch on around the building. I decided he needed a shirt, and now his message is not only audible but visible, too.

Putting on this HAT: To me, it's a simple little saying, but what does it mean? It means he is ready. He is positive and he is enthusiastic. He has a *How can I help you?* attitude and an *I'm going to get the job done* mindset. How do you respond when people greet you? Do they respond "Oooh, yeah," or do they respond with "Oh, no!"? I think it's so important that we energize others with our words and in our actions. A simple smile and a boost of energy with an "Oooh, yeah" can go a long way.

I'm grateful for Donald Burke and the many talented and caring educators and people in the community of Port Jervis. Continue to celebrate and inspire your community in the little and big things that people are doing. #Ooohyeah!

It's Okay to Say *Love*
Jay Billy

I truly love what I do, and I don't mind letting people know. I know sometimes I can drive people crazy with my enthusiasm and passion, but I feel blessed to be able to do what I do every single day. I also recognize that not everyone, including students, come to school fully in love with being there each and every day. The fact is, we don't always know what is going on in our students' homes, and as close as we get to them, they don't always communicate their problems.

In my first year here at BFS, we had quite a few students who, some would say, were hard to love. They were a little out of control and not always nice to each other. As I got to know and understand them, I started to earn their trust by talking to them and showing them that I cared for them. I invited them in to have lunch with me, I talked to them in the hallways, and I treated them fairly and respectfully. I also showed an interest in their lives outside of school. It was evident that some of them had quite a few traumatic experiences in their lives and that many of them used their behavior to communicate in negative ways. This is when you need to love these students even more.

Whether we are disciplining our students or having lunch with them, I feel it's important that they know I love them. Students who need our love often tell us in the most creative and distressing ways. It's our job to love them anyway. And, it's okay to say it.

One day, I was in the middle of a crisis where a student had lost control, and I was sitting on the floor with him, trying to calm him and keep him from hurting himself or someone else. Usually, when students see me in the middle of this type of situation, they will just walk by. In this situation, one of my toughest kids thought this was the perfect time to come up and tell me something. I, rudely, told her to get away from me and the situation, knowing it would set my student off even more. After things had settled, I went and found her and apologized for being so direct and not having the time for her. Do you know what she said to me? "Don't worry about it, Mr. Billy—I know you love me anyway."

That's right. I do love her and all of my students. So . . . I make a point of telling them and showing them. Oftentimes, when students are leaving after a tough day or even when I've just had to discipline a student, I'll remind them that I love them, saying, "Love you all," at the end of the day as they leave or at the end of an assembly. It's okay to say the word "*love*."

Putting on this HAT: So often, many of the kids we see in front of us don't come to school feeling loved or valued. It is our job to make sure that we become that person who they know loves them for who they are and wants the best for them, no matter the situation. If you're uncomfortable saying it, make sure that they can at least feel it. When they feel the love, they know that you are with them and are there to make a difference for them. In the end, everyone wants to be loved. You may be the one who can give that to a student.

Signs of Maturity
Brian McCann

During an annual parent-teacher conference event that was held in mid-November, I was making my rounds throughout the evening. I used this event for high-school families to see me in person, greet them, answer any questions, and hopefully troubleshoot any pressing issue.

I was in the cafeteria, checking in with a bake sale, when a parent approached me.

"Do you have a minute, Mr. McCann?" this parent asked. I knew the mom as one of my own English students almost two decades before and had had some minimal interaction with her as a mother of a student. Her daughter struggled to find success in high school during her first few years but recently seemed to have learned to successfully navigate the road after a few bumps.

Her daughter was the first student that I took a picture with on my #PositiveSignThursday debut that fall. On the first Thursday of the school year, I stood outside the school as students got off the bus or were dropped off in the front. The sign stated "YOU ARE FABULOUS." Shelley and I took a great picture.

On a whim, I had a staff member take a picture of me with a student and the sign. Later that morning, I posted the picture on social media. The picture went viral around the school and community, and kicked off a six-year commitment to promoting positivity throughout the school.

When I was challenged to continue this the next week, I again took a picture with Shelley, whose mom had dropped her off. By the time I committed to every Thursday, Shelley and I decided that we would take a picture together every week to document her senior year.

"Do you have a minute, Mr. McCann?" I was transformed back to reality, and a flurry of potential problems exploded in my mind. Mom seemed serious. Really serious.

"I just want to . . ." The scene paused for a moment in my mind. *What did I do wrong? How can I make this better? How will I fix this?*

"I just want to *thank you* for taking the pictures with my girl. She hasn't always found high school to be an easy place, but now she looks forward to Thursday."

Mom went on to tell me that she prepares her outfit in advance and makes sure that she is up early to do her hair. All because she is taking a picture with the principal and a sign.

Shelley finished her senior year *successfully* with many photos with the principal that flooded social media each week. We even took one on the football field after she was awarded her high-school diploma.

More than the signs, more than the photos, more than the social-media posts was the relationship that was built with this student during her senior year.

It literally costs nothing but, in the end, was probably the most valuable strategy to get Shelley on track.

Since her graduation, I've only seen her once and shared her joy when she told me that she was to be a new mom. Last spring, I bumped into her mother again. She reminded me of the close relationship we'd forged during her senior year because of a paper sign and some pictures. Shelley had a new blessing on the way.

Putting on this HAT: Do not underestimate the power of relationships to motivate children to successful closure.

Third-Party Compliments
Jay Billy

Through the pandemic, one of the things that we became even more aware of was taking care of our students and their social-emotional needs. The inability to connect and have those day-to-day exchanges and experiences made some of our students lose the ability to understand how others are feeling and also how they are feeling. Many students lost their own ability to feel good about themselves and those around them.

As we wrestle with how to help our students feel loved and connected on a daily basis, we also consider it a key component for making our school culture a place where students want to be. Last spring, we did a survey that involved students, staff, and our community. This survey was to measure the culture and gain an understanding of the needs of our students. One of the results of the survey was that it seemed that staff and families had a higher estimate of our student self-esteem than the students themselves felt. So, obviously, one of our school goals this year is to increase students' self-worth and self-esteem using a self-made inventory. We assessed students early in the year and will reassess them at the end of the year.

In the past, I've encouraged teachers to do periodic check-ins with their students to judge how students are feeling about themselves. It can be as simple as asking the students in the class, "Who is Mr. Billy's favorite student?" "Who is Mr. Billy's least-favorite student?" By doing this, we as educators can see how students perceive us and how they think they are perceived by us. If every student in the class thinks they are my favorite student, then I'm doing a really good job of making them feel valued. If every student in the classroom thinks that "Samantha" is my favorite student, then I really need to look at how I'm coming across as the classroom leader and consider changing how I treat "Samantha" or better yet, how I treat and respond to *all* of the students. If every student recognizes that "Tommy" is Mr. Billy's least-favorite student, then I really need to change the way I speak to and about "Tommy." I need to re-think everything about what I am doing and find ways to lift up "Tommy" in the eyes of his peers.

Another way of checking in can be to do a quick survey, asking the students, "Who is your best friend in the classroom?" By doing this, you are basically checking the pulse of the classroom. Obviously and especially at the elementary level, BFFs can change on a daily basis. but sometimes it's good to see how those changes are affecting the entire classroom and individual students. If "Sid" and "Sara" were best friends the first two months of school and no longer consider each other that, and you've noticed a change in behavior in one or both of them, then you could have some ideas why that behavior has changed and maybe even need to provide some counseling or restorative work.

Recently, I was at a conference where I heard about something called, "Third-Party Compliments." I watched a video of high-school students sharing written compliments they'd received from their peers, and you could just see some of them light up. Some students cried when they read a very nice compliment from another student directed at them. It was so kind and joyful and really touched their hearts and the hearts of us who were witnessing this. The cool thing about giving compliments is that the person giving the compliment also gets a sense of joy and happiness by giving it. It goes both ways!

I wondered how this would look at the elementary level, but I figured I'd give it a shot. We hold monthly all-school meetings, and we have been working on all school norms and behaviors. We had spent the last month remembering to use good manners, and we've really seen it make a difference. At this all-school meeting, I introduced the concept of Third-Party Compliments. I shared a video of students getting compliments and how it made them feel. Then I explained that we were starting this at our school.

Putting on this HAT: I have made up a short form (and revised it numerous times), but students can use any piece of paper. They are to write a compliment to a student or teacher. In it, they are not only to give a compliment but also explain it. For our kindergarten students, I am looking for more than, "I like your shoes." I want to know what it is that this person has done to make you happy, feel good, or smile. For our youngest students, they can give the words to the teacher, and the teacher can write them. Our older students can have the teacher look at them if they are unsure how to spell or make sense. There is a box next to the office door that students can drop these compliments in, and then I will deliver them. Students can sign their name to it, but they don't have to.

I made up some blank copies of the form and put them in each classroom box, but, as I said, any piece of paper will do. Little did I know that I was giving myself another full-time job. Within days, I had hundreds of compliments to deliver. I try to do it early in the morning, but there are so many. I want the students to read them out loud so their classmates can really take it in. When reading these compliments, the students light up and smile because they know they've done something special or kind and that someone recognized them for this. Now, every time I walk into classrooms, students are looking for me to deliver Third-Party Compliments, and it is one of the best parts of my day.

Thanks to Scott Wisniewski, Assistant Principal at Wayne Valley High School, and New Jersey Visionary Assistant Principal of the Year 2022, for sharing this idea.

Advisories: Something You Don't Know About Me
Brian McCann

Like Jay Billy's "Third Party Compliments" in the last chapter, sometimes an unexpected shared sentiment can help transform a student from feeling alone to feeling like a member of a community.

Advisories are formal opportunities for teachers and students to make connections that may not have occurred otherwise. Blessed with a small, manageable school population, we started an advisory program at the high school in preparation for our impending accreditation. After a one-year pilot, we were able to break up the entire school into small communities of approximately 12 students that would meet regularly with the same adult in the building throughout a four-year high school career.

These small groups ensured that *every* student had at least one adult in the building who got to know them personally and would be a resource for them throughout their secondary journey.

Activities in advisory varied.

A few times a year, we would poll the entire community on a question. Using color-coded Post-It notes with the faculty and assigning each class a different color, teachers and students would record responses, and then we would publish them in a common area.

Questions might be: "What would you like to do better in Term II?" "What do you hope to do in five years?" "What is your goal for this school year?" Since the opportunity to respond was done in a supervised advisory, systems were in place to make sure that all members at school that day responded.

One of the most profound questions that was posed was the following: *What is something that people don't know about you?* The responses were humbling.

Under the shield of anonymity, people were brutally honest about something that they kept close to them. Many students indicated some sort of anxiety. Others told about pressures from their peers or family. Some shared private battles that they were fighting outside of the school day.

The statement that shocked me the most was: *No one knows that my son is an addict.* Wow!! This person's courage to share this info—*and* the strength to be a servant leader while things are not rosy at home—are amazing.

After we finished the bulletin board that was strategically placed in the cafeteria, I watched the students and adults during the next weeks. Many visited the board to read the responses. Some used a more private time after school to view.

What the Post-It notes did was help solidify a community.

Putting on this HAT: What better way to make school connections than to establish experiences so that students—and teachers—do not feel isolated. When community members read responses and think to themselves, *That's me, too,* the feeling of being alone begins to lessen.

I often reflect on the teacher who shared about a family member's struggles. I think about how many families in the school are affected by chains of addiction. I thought about how many of us put on strong faces at school when situations spiral out of our control at home.

Just knowing there were, indeed, others who experience this brought me some solace. I felt a deeper connection to the community—a connection that was the result of a small piece of paper.

Little things can have a profound personal impact. And in this, I learned a little something more about myself.

Wow! The Flowers Look Beautiful
Andrew Marotta

When I arrived at Port Jervis High School in the spring of '05, the 9/11 memorial flower bed was bare. It was just dirt that was stepped on, and worn. When I asked about it, the most common answer was, "Oh, the kids will just ruin it," or "The kids will destroy it, so we don't bother."

Don't bother! What? Don't bother! No way. Of course, bother! Of course, we need to act on this. It was the 9/11 garden, and it was right out in front of the school. It had to be addressed.

Seeing the barren garden each day reminded me of the story in New York City when my Dad was the community board chair. He was leading a meeting about putting a fountain in an area in New York City that historically was not the nicest area. He and the other leaders wanted to beautify it and make it more appealing, more attractive. When he threw the idea out about the fountain, people made all kinds of reasons why *not* to do it: vandalism, the cost, the maintenance, the freezing, etc. People kept bringing up that people would destroy it and ruin it. My Dad slammed his fist down on the table, and sternly and firmly said loudly, "Then we'll fix it! We will not allow vandalism to stop us from beautifying our community."

Putting on this HAT: We just did it. We scraped together some small funding, received some donations, asked for volunteers, and just did it. We planted flowers not only in that small area but also the entire front of the school. Staff, students, and community members all pitched in and beautified the area. When people came onto campus, so many greeted me and others with, "Wow, the flowers look beautiful!"

It was the most rewarding compliment, and just like in my Dad's meeting when people were talking about the bad things that could happen to the fountain, we had a similar reaction. And when the flowers were damaged, which wasn't often, we fixed them. When they died, we got more. When they needed watering, we watered them. It was awesome and a great change for our district and community. I was very proud to be part of bringing this HAT to Port Jervis schools.

Play that Funky Music
Jay Billy

Music is a universal language. No matter the age of your students or the type of music your staff likes or listens to. It's hard to be in a bad mood when there is music playing. If our goal is really to have staff, students, and families running *into* our school instead of *away*, we need to do things on a daily basis to get them to wonder. Wonder what is it that we're going to do tomorrow. Wonder *What will they come up with to get me excited about the day?*

Believe it or not, there are some days when I'm not all that excited about getting things going in the morning. Those are the days that the "jammy pack" comes out. The "jammy pack" is a fanny pack with speakers and Bluetooth in it. Then I pair my speakers with some music on my phone that gets me excited. My playlists could be from the holidays or '90s jams, or sometimes I'll do a Kidzbop medley for the kids. I turn the music up loud, head outside, and greet the students as they get off the bus or walk down the hill. The cool thing is, sometimes, you'll see the kids start moving to the music as well. They'll get off the buses and dance or move a little. It puts a smile on their faces and often a smile on the faces of the other staff outside with me. People notice and expect it. Not every day, but people expect me to do the unexpected in order to make school amazing for the kids.

It's funny, but as we worked our way out of the pandemic, we were coming back to our first day of hybrid learning. Students hadn't been in the building in many months, and there were a lot of restrictions and rules for students and staff to follow. I was outside, as normal, helping and greeting kids, checking on masking requirements and spacing, and being visible for the families. Things went pretty well, and, once everyone was in school to start the day, I returned to my desk, where I saw an email from a parent who'd had other students in our school previously. The email explained how they were "disappointed" at our opening, because *normally* I had music playing, and I generated a party atmosphere for the opening. They said their child was looking forward to coming back and that everything seemed so "sterile." They specifically mentioned the lack of music and celebration. As I sat there at my desk, I realized that, because of all the intricacies of reopening, I had not given the kids my best. I focused on the safety issues and ignored that I was responsible for making memories and delivering a school that kids can't wait to get into. I quickly wrote an apology email to the parent and set the stage for a better opening the next day.

The following day and for the entire week, I had the music blaring, signs up welcoming students back, and lots of fist bumps for all who wanted them (with hand sanitizer right inside the door.) During that time, I realized the power that music has on feelings and mood in our school and in the world.

Putting on this HAT: Playing music is an easy way to put smiles on faces, get kids and staff moving, and bring your own mood and emotions up. Whether you have a small music box or a "jammy pack" when you play the music, it makes you feel better. You don't have to do it every day and you don't have to blare it from the building speakers, but spice things up and have some fun with it. Let kids choose the music. Let staff choose. Find some themes. Just make it move, and be careful to make sure that it is all kid-friendly.

Carry the Banner for Your School and Community
Andrew Marotta

I heard the great Jimmy Casas speak at the National Principals Convention in Boston, Massachusetts. Jimmy is a school leader, author, mentor, and friend. I admire his message, style, and leadership. That day, one message in particular resonated with me: Carry the Banner for your school and community. He continued to share about the many things this means and how you can go about carrying out this act, this HAT. I loved it and became even more enthused to be the Principal of Port Jervis schools.

At events, I wasn't just an attendee. I was there carrying the banner for the schools and community. At Eagle Scout ceremonies, funerals, school-board meetings, graduation parties, and on other occasions, I was carrying the banner. At local parades, I was proud to wear my Port gear and represent the schools. Now, as a national speaker, I proudly represent Port Jervis schools and speak about the great things happening in our schools.

The HAT, carrying the banner, means so much and is so many things. Do you wear your school's gear out and about? Do you advocate for the best programs, the best equipment, and the best staff for your school? Are you a beacon of positivity and hope for your school and community? The questions and opportunities can go on and on to carry the banner for your school and community.

Putting on this HAT: Go for it. You don't need a position, a title, or permission to do this HAT. It is a moving target, a different act, HAT each day, and a continued path. It is service, it is public, and it is being part of something greater than yourself. Your school needs you and more like you to help carry the banner for so many in so many different ways. Thank you for carrying the banner. Thank you, Jimmy Casas, for introducing me to this HAT. It has meant so much to me and my school and community.

Send All the Shoes You Have
Andrew Marotta

There was a shoe company that sent two salespeople to two different remote islands looking to sell shoes to the natives. Each salesperson arrived at their separate locations and got to work. The first person, after being there just one day, called the company and said, "Come pick me up. This is a waste of time. There are a lot of people here, but no one is wearing shoes."

The second salesperson called shortly afterward and enthusiastically asked to speak to the CEO of the company. Once connected, she yelled into the phone, "Send me everything you got. No one here wears shoes, and there is a ton of opportunity here!"

Putting on this HAT: This happens each day in schools around the world. It is all about how we look at things, the lens through which we see the world. A heartfelt act for a teacher or student is believing in them. It is giving them a chance. Don't we talk about growth scores all the time with kids? Teacher evaluations with test scores? A growth mindset, a positive outlook, and the E + R = O mentality. Event plus Response equals Outcome.

It wasn't that no one wore shoes on the islands, yet it was the salesperson's *response* that produced the amazing outcome. Think about the student with low reading scores. How do we treat that young person? Is there a mindset that they'll never read, or do we look at it that there is great potential, an amazing opportunity? Look for these HATS in your school, and start selling those shoes!

CHAPTER 9

TIPPING YOUR HATS

PORT Center and PORT Center Spotlight
Andrew Marotta

The pandemic brought a lot of items to the forefront of our work as educators: inequities, distractions, technology, engagement, and more. One thing it made me do was video announcements. No longer could I just pop on the loudspeaker and read the announcements for the day. When we returned to in-person instruction post-pandemic, we decided to keep the video announcements once a week on Fridays and make them special, extended announcements called "PORT Center" (my district in Port Jervis [New York] City School District). A staff member made a cool logo, and off we went. We were able  to record these, and post them for the students, staff, and community . . . and it really caught on. Kids wanted to present on PORT Center, sing songs, share their awards and recognitions, and more. It became a fun, different way to share out information with the school.

We took it a step deeper and started PORT Center Spotlight: a short interview with a staff, student, or community member to highlight something about them—approximately an 8–10 minute interview that we recorded and shared out. Positive, good news is contagious, and we should spread it more. This was a free way to spread the good news about our most important asset in schools: the people!

Putting on this HAT: I want to thank my secretary for creating these awesome images. She is so talented, and, when I presented these ideas to her, *Bam!* She ran with them. Try it (video announcements and interviews). If you like this, you just have to start. Get the right people on board, schedule it, and go. Maybe you are introverted, or maybe you are nervous about being on camera, or just plain ol' uncomfortable with it. It doesn't have to be you on the camera all the time, either. Have the kids or other staff be the stars of the videos. Some schools have a whole class and production studio to make this all work. What's the end result? Positive promotion of your school community for many to see.

From "Trash" to "Bank": Snow Day #1
Brian McCann

I'm embarrassed that our snow-day videos started in spite. I was home one snowy winter day when school had been canceled, and I saw a brief story on the local TV news station.

A high school principal had produced and starred in a snow-day video set to a popular song. The news anchors went wild for the story and told us how great it was.

I thought it was okay, perhaps highly mediocre. The singing wasn't that great, and the video didn't tell any story.

When I went back to school after this pause, I spoke of the news story to my theater teacher. He had seen it as well, and we started the trash talk.

We could do so much better.

The conversation broadened to include our video teacher, who shared in our negativity. We were so much more talented than this video. We could produce a much better one than that.

There was lots of *talk* that year about how great we were. No *action*. No *plan* to produce. Just a lot of empty words.

When the next school year started, I brought these two teachers together with me and asked them if they wanted to make a snow-day video. We agreed that we had the resources, and the brainstorming began.

The scenario would be simple: a principal would get an alert from his superintendent that there is no school, and he must then make the announcement.

At the time of the pre-production, the high school was wrapping up its fall musical, Kander and Ebb's *Chicago*. Taking the music

201

from its opening number, I jotted down a few lines that changed the intent of the song from "All That Jazz" to "All That Snow."

I bandied some ideas about for creating a production number, using the sets and costumes from the show, while meeting separately with the video teacher on solidifying a frame for the story.

We agreed that the most important aspect of the video at this point was the surprise: we would tell no one we were making it. When our theater teacher suggested a small ensemble of dancers, we solicited high-school thespians with the understanding that this was a secret project.

We called our clandestine venture "Project Voldemort," inspired by the villain from *Harry Potter* whose name must not be spoken. We could use this code term without raising any eyebrows or suspicions about the pending video shoot. Our video teacher storyboarded the narrative. The drama teacher found some music online to accompany the short video. Singers were solicited to help record backup vocals with me. Dancers from our current production of *Chicago* were selected, and the date was determined for shooting. *Chicago* closed with a Sunday matinee: we would shoot the next day after school in the auditorium, using the production's set before it was dismantled.

On that Monday, we put together—in about 90 minutes—an experience that would change how the nation looked at our school. Using our own pre-recorded tracks, we taped our first snow-day video (and even used two old snow machines that were in theater storage from a production of *A Christmas Carol* a few years back).

Putting on this HAT: All kidding and bad-mouthing aside, this special project brought together administrators, teachers, and students who modeled collaboration and risk-taking. Projects like this could not even be attempted if there were not a healthy culture and existing positive relationships already in the school.

We waited patiently through the driest and "unsnowiest" November and December to date. When would "Project Voldemort" be unleashed?

The Debut and a Call from NPR
Brian McCann

Since our planning, production, and post-production were completed before the end of October, those involved in "Project Voldemort" *almost* forgot about this project. Given the driest November and December in recent memory, we left school for our December break with our snow-day video being just a Term I memory. New adventures in the New Year could soon overshadow this experience.

Frankly, we almost forgot that we did it.

When we returned to school, local TV weather forecasters were beginning to talk about the possibility of some accumulating snow later in the week. I went to see my drama and video teachers early the next morning, during our first period of instruction. "Looks like it might be a Voldemort Day later this week," I said.

Most students ignored this cryptic message. A few, however, popped their head up and smiled. They know that a *possibility* might exist for unleashing our snow-day video.

The weather forecast became more grave as the week continued, with at least a foot of snow expected with our first Nor'easter of the season. The outlook became so grave that the superintendent of schools canceled the night before.

This announcement set us in motion.

We unveiled our snow-day video at 6 a.m. on Facebook and Twitter. We tagged all the local TV news stations in the Providence and Boston markets so that broadcasters would have a chance to showcase our work in an optimally timely manner. This is what we sent them:

https://bit.ly/HATSAllThatSnow

Not only did this video go viral, but we also heard from many of our high-school alumni about how proud they were. People kept retweeting the video and sharing it on their Facebook feeds. We were featured on many news segments and even had an inquiry from a nationally syndicated talk show to celebrate our video.

The most important message for the public to receive from this video was not that there was no school, but the realization that a project like this could not exist in a culture that was not healthy, progressive, and relationship-oriented. It modeled vulnerability and risk-taking, showing that this high school could be a fun place to learn.

Soon we had thousands of hits on YouTube and were creating quite a buzz in the community.

Fast-forward a year. People still mentioned the video from time to time, but it wasn't until my administrative assistant popped her head into my office one morning that I truly remembered its impact.

"Mr. McCann," she said, "National Public Radio is on the phone for you. Do you want to take it?"

A pit in my stomach blossomed. Why does NPR want to talk to me? I convinced myself that they probably wanted some local reaction to a school problem, like vaping, which had been in the news. I steeled myself and took the call.

The reporter was not interested in vaping or test scores or school security. The reporter was doing a feature on how schools had taken cancellation announcements to a new level and wanted to speak with me.

Suddenly I was *very* interested in taking the call.

The interview was part of that afternoon's larger feature story that was also curated on the NPR webpage:

https://bit.ly/HATSNPR

Within 24 hours, we had more than 70,000 YouTube hits. We also were gifted with a tremendously favorable response across the country.

Putting on this HAT: Lots of lessons were learned in this experience. News outlets are desperate for good stories to promote, but schools must do a lot of the work to get these ideas on the air. Once again, you need to have relationships in place so that trust can be built between you and the media.

Risks like this can instill a sense of pride in your community and help guide outsiders' perspectives of your school into a positive direction. The students who were part of this project still talk about the positive excitement they felt when "Project Voldemort" was debuted initially.

The gauntlet had been thrown for future cohorts of students to engage in next year's snow-day video.

Building Culture by Building Interest: Snow Day #2
Brian McCann

The overwhelming reception to our first snow-day video resulted in a buzz about when we would produce a second. A lot of work goes into both the pre-and post-production of these videos, far more time than to actually record the raw footage. I'll be honest: we had grand dreams of making many more that year, but the reality of running, teaching, and attending school took all of our time and energy.

In addition to staff and students finding great pride in the video, it was mentioned all the time through the end of the school year: at regional meetings, at a sports event, in the market, and even at a wake for a family friend.

And the mention was always followed by a smile. Our goal was met: to produce a product we were proud of, to foster a sense of community in the building, and to bring some fleeting happiness to those who viewed it.

The adult team agreed to reconvene at the start of the next year to plan our next attack. It would no longer be a secret project; it quickly became something that the community expected and was looking forward to.

Deciding on a show-tune medley with a few, different, quick vignettes, we included more students and paid tribute to the musicals *Anything Goes, Chicago, Dear Evan Hansen,* and *Jersey Boys.* We used costumes from our theater's extensive wardrobe collection and partnered with a local tux company for formalwear for one segment in return for some onscreen credit.

Pre-production took longer, since we were dealing with multiple songs in multiple locations with numerous cast members. Adults wrote, revised and envisioned the project. We tried using some new spaces at the high school outside of the auditorium. It was funny to watch the reaction of students who were in the school after the formal school day when we were taping segments. You could tell that they were interested in the project but were not surprised that it was occurring. Our second project managed to get some faculty as well in the opening moments, helping to spread enthusiasm for this project.

We even had some parents who were early for a game watch us do a few "takes" and commented on how wonderful it was that we could do collaborative projects like this.

The beauty of this event is that these parents will share the story with other families, and the positivity in the community will continue to spread.

In the end, we had to wait until March for a snow day, if memory serves. Here is our second effort that we shared with the community:

https://bit.ly/HATSSnowDay

Putting on this HAT: Our second video resulted in more accolades for our school. The most resonating comment was that only a school with a healthy culture could effectively pull off something like this. All of the work in building relationships with a variety of stakeholders pays off when you again model risk-taking and vulnerability for your community. NPR might not have highlighted this event, but we showed the digital world we were not a one-hit-wonder.

Social Media for Recognition of Greatness
Jay Billy

Early on in my career, I didn't understand the importance of social media in education. I really didn't get it. What was the purpose?

In 2011, I attended a workshop in our district where we learned about using Twitter. At that time, I still didn't get it. In 2013, I attended the National Association of Elementary School Principals Conference in Baltimore. The final keynote address was given by Todd Whitaker, a noted educational author and leader. One of the first things he said was, "If you're not on Twitter, you are missing out on some of the best professional development and learning there is." At that moment, I realized that I needed to engage and connect. After figuring out my two-year-old password, I began to follow Todd Whitaker. I began to engage, retweet, and follow others that he followed. I began to interact and learn on a daily basis. I began to share my thoughts and ideas. Most of all, I began to share the ideas and cool things happening in our classrooms.

I use social media for a number of reasons. The first reason is to learn. When you are on social media with other great educators throughout the world, you can learn what they are doing and what they have done, and share resources. The second reason I like using social media is that it connects me to greatness on a daily basis. The third reason is that posting things on social media holds me accountable. If I share something that I've done or say I'm going to do, there are people out there who will fact-check me and verify. It pushes me to be transparent. Finally, I want to be the one who is telling the story of our school and classrooms. By posting classroom activities, pictures, and lessons, people can really see what is going on daily.

One piece of telling the story of our school and classrooms through social media is the fact that I'm usually posting things that I'm proud of or I think are exceptional. So, if I come into a teacher's classroom and share activities and pictures, it's because

I think what I see is good practice. Teachers who are also on social media will see my tweets or posts and feel recognized and supported. It's a simple way of giving positive feedback for the greatness I see in classrooms. If I'm tweeting, then I'm impressed. Other teachers will see that I tweeted something from this classroom and reach out for ideas or shared plans. People across the country will reach out and ask, "Hey, what is that you are doing?" What better way to validate good practices than to have others ask for your ideas? What better way to ensure that good practices are repeated than this type of public feedback? What gives a teacher more validation than someone reaching out and saying, "I'm stealing that."

School leaders use social media for a lot of reasons, but bragging about their staff and the amazing things they are doing with students is a meaningful way to harness the power of social media for good. Make a teacher's day. Tweet from their classroom.

Putting on this HAT: Social media can be scary and can become overwhelming. Don't look at it that way. Think of it as an opportunity to share what is awesome about your school, and go to the places where our families are. As a leader, you want to be in the room with the smartest people you know or want to know. Join Twitter, Instagram, and Facebook. Venture into TikTok if you are really brave. There are educational communities on all of these platforms. Start small if this is too much for you—just one tweet a day from a classroom. Make up a hashtag for your school so others know where to go to find you. Believe me, if you begin to tweet from my school, I am proud that you think what I'm doing is worthy. Do that for your teachers.

The Tweets
Brian McCann

The highlight of being part of the audience at the Tweets, an annual high-school ceremony that celebrates local filmmaking, was not seeing myself on screen or awaiting the outcome of the acting award for which I was nominated. It wasn't the fresh popcorn, the red carpet outside the theater, or the local paparazzi who snapped picture after picture of our guests, who were all dressed up. It wasn't the packed auditorium or the anticipation of a local celebration.

The highlight for me was learning what at least seven of my teachers did over Spring Break.

The Tweets were a fundraising idea brought to me by the video teacher, who advocated for a platform to celebrate our hard-working filmmakers. And since so many students and teachers are part of these local films, the stakeholders deserved a star-studded forum to laud the best of the best.

"Mental Math" was a big hit for two consecutive years before, about a teacher with a superpower to destroy his students' love of math—and the villain's ultimate demise. The film was pure villainous evil from a math perspective, and pure camp and hilarity from the point of view of the audience.

Part 3 was scheduled this year. The audience could not wait.

The black-and-white title frame looked remarkably like a 1972 film classic.

The haunting trumpets of iconic theme music.

A pervading visual palette of soft tones of orange, sienna, and mahogany.

We were watching a tribute to Francis Ford Coppola's *The Godfather*. The cast was made up of teachers with common ethnicity: Palmisciano, Palladino, Pasquariello, Puccio, and Lucca. It was a meeting of the family to discern what had all gone wrong in Part 2 of "Mental Math."

I never have laughed more.

And then my amusement quickly transitioned to awe when I realized that these educators gave up a good chunk of their Spring Break to film. They willingly returned to school over Break for a higher cause: student art.

This episode of the film is a reflection of the selflessness of educators in our community. Teachers who go beyond the final bell of the school day. Teachers who will model vulnerability and, perhaps, inspire the student who might be on the fence about taking a risk at school. These are teachers who deserve a standing ovation each day!

Check out the entire Case High Media Channel here:

https://bit.ly/HATSTheTweets

The "Mental Math" series is under "Playlists."

Putting on this HAT: A school community that has not prioritized culture and climate will find it difficult to grow. Teachers and students have to know they are safe to try new things, and sometimes we need to fail forward. The educators who were part of this *Godfather* tribute will forever continue their student influence since it has been captured, curated, and celebrated in video forever.

Snow Day-a-Mia
Brian McCann

Theater is huge at my school. One man, Tom Marcello, oversaw the program for 40 years until he passed away after an illness. As a student at the high school that I led, I was in his first production. He was succeeded by a graduate and theater alumnus of the high school who took all of the good work he did over 40 years and then made it even better.

Our production of the hit musical *Mamma Mia* had a cast and crew of about 300 students from the town. Not too bad for a high school's 550-student population. So, when we began to talk of our third snow-day video, our team of adults decided to capitalize on the popularity of an ABBA-inspired event. This one would embrace even more students than Year #2.

With our theater teacher, I put together a mashup of ABBA tunes all around the conceit that our school couldn't wait for a snow day. We would use a series of school interior and exterior shots, ending with a big dance finale onstage. The trouble was that our story takes place in a snowstorm, yet is being filmed during a warm, sunny autumn in New England.

Again, our snow machines came in very handy. Using a base that is very much like soap flakes, we recreated a storm that the principal could drive his car in and enter the school from.

We filmed it on two successive occasions, using lots of theater students who had not been in the videos in the past.

What we didn't count on was the wind.

A persistent wind.

Wind that blew the snow/soapsuds onto half the cars in the faculty parking lot.

Soapy *teacher* cars in the faculty parking lot.

There were two blessings, however. There are very few classrooms with windows on that side of the building. And one room with a direct exit to the parking lot is the theater classroom.

That has a sink.

In a true instance of collaboration, theater students, the teacher, and the principal found as many buckets and containers as we could, filling them with water. We began a bucket brigade—passing the water from one person to the next—to remove the residue before the end of the school day. We had about 45 minutes to get it right.

The high school's faculty parking lot looked like the set of a "Three Stooges" episode gone wrong, with streams of soapy water running across the asphalt. By the close of school, the soap had dissipated, with little trace of the snow-day video remnants from an hour before.

Thankfully, I received no feedback whatsoever on this from any faculty member. I wonder if they even knew what was going on.

As for the video, it was wrapped up well before we broke for the December holidays. There was no snow day that year, however, and on Friday, March 13, 2020, we left school for a "two-week pause" that turned into the rest of the school year because of the pandemic.

As a gift to the school community, I aired the video to our community later that month. These were uncertain times at this point, and spirits needed some lift:

https://bit.ly/HATSSnowDayaMia

Putting on this HAT: Sometimes the intent that you've planned for doesn't come to fruition. The pandemic taught us all about flexibility and alternate pathways. The third snow-day video was no different. I think Tom Marcello would have been proud of the video, its changing intent, and that we literally cleaned up our mess without a scandal.

Fence Messages
Jay Billy

Many schools have a sign or some type of messaging out front of their buildings that tells families and the public about upcoming events, reminds viewers of important dates, or provides inspirational messages. Unfortunately, our school does not have a sign to post about our school. These types of signs can be pretty expensive, and some require the school or district to get special permits and city variances to have them posted. Also, many schools often have fences around their property, playgrounds, or parking areas.

My school has a chain-link fence in front of the school, circling a small play area for our kindergarten and preschool students. The fence is often the first thing you see when you drive by or come into the bus loop. This fence serves its purpose—to keep people out—yet still allows you to see into the area. I often see schools hang signs on their fences, and we do this as well when there is something big happening in the district. But, on a day-to-day basis, the fence is usually left blank.

One day when I was scrolling through Twitter, I saw that someone used small paper cups in their fence to spell out words. An idea was born. I went to the store and purchased a couple of packs of three-ounce plastic cups and began to figure out how to use them to share inspiration and make announcements. It's a way of messaging that catches the eye of those who come to our school every day, but also those passing by. Sometimes the messages are relevant to the time of year, such as, "Happy Holidays," or, "Here Comes the Snow." Other times, I use meaningful sayings to remind our students, staff, and the public about what we stand for. Things like, "No Place for Hate," or, "Making Every Day Amazing," have been posted. I've used the fence to congratulate our Teacher of the Year or to welcome families to "Back-to-School Night."

As with any HAT, making the changes in the fence signs becomes a chore and another duty that sometimes becomes overwhelming. I often wonder if people even read them or if anyone notices when I change the signs, but when the pandemic hit in 2020, I decided to take the signs down. I had used the same cups for almost 8 months; they were old and cracking, and I had the time to clean things up. So, I took the sign down off the fence and left it down. There were no students and staff in the school building; everyone was learning and working from home, so I figured I'd give it a break.

About one week later, I was working in my office when I received an email from an address that I didn't recognize. I don't often open emails from unknown people, but this one had the subject: Fence messages. When I opened this message, it was just a short note from a community member who said:

"Dear Mr. Billy,

My name is _____ and I live _____, not far from your school. I know this pandemic must be tough on you and all of your students and their families. I hope that things get better soon and that we can return to normal. I'm writing to you today because I walk by your school every day as part of my daily exercise routine, and I noticed you've taken down your signs on the fence. I miss reading what you have up there, and I was hoping that you'd put the messages up again. I think it would be good for the community, and I know it would be good for me.

"Thank you for your consideration,

_____"

Upon reading this, I immediately went out and put up a new sign on the fence. I didn't realize the powerful effect that positive messaging had on the community. When I first put up the messages, I just did it for our school, and now it had become part of who we were. During the pandemic, it became even more important to spread positivity and keep the community informed. It's a small gesture for an unknown impact on the entire school community.

Putting on this HAT: You never know the impact that the things you do for your school can have on the entire community. I think of Ted Lasso and his simple sign, "Believe," over the door of the team room. People see it every day but don't really think about it in depth until it's not there. When people see positive messages coming from the school they come to every day, it provides a glimpse of positivity or sparks a thought that may change their day for the better. Keep spreading the messages!

CONCLUSION

HATS OFF TO YOU!

Absorb Chaos, Create Calm, and Provide Hope
Andrew Marotta

This was the title of the last chapter of my book *Tales from the Hardwood*. The excerpt was authored by the former National Coordinator of NCAA basketball officials, J.D. Collins. When I interviewed J.D. on my podcast, #ELB Education Leadership and Beyond, he shared this concept when I asked him to describe his job as national coordinator. You can view the interview here:

https://bit.ly/HATSJDCollins

In designing and deciding on the final message of this book about HATS: Heartfelt Acts for Teachers, Students, and Staff, we reflected deeply on many of the topics, tools, and tips in this book. We also thought about the school year and all of the ups and downs that educators face each and every day, each and every period.

In the end, it comes down to *support*. How can we support each other as educators, our students in their learning, and ourselves in our wellness? It can be a tough road sometimes. I believe this HAT is all-encompassing to what educators are facing: Absorb chaos, create calm, and provide hope. Let's break it down.

Absorb chaos: There are many twists and turns, hurdles, and speed bumps working in schools. Staff turnover, social media, day-to-day working with students, negative attacks on educators, mandates, technology, and more, more, and more. Absorb it, don't deflect it. Work through it. Take the blame, and pass the credit. We need stars like you, with the unique ability to absorb it all to continue to move our kids, schools, and education forward.

Create Calm: How can we create this in our districts and schools? Sometimes it feels chaotic; how can we make it calmer? How can we become more proactive as opposed to reactive? Here are a few suggestions to help create calm in your world:

- Schedule it: Be organized with your schedule, and plan it out.

- Share the vision: What is it you are trying to accomplish, and how are you communicating these goals and visions to your teams?

- Consistency: People thrive in situations where there is consistency. They know what to expect: how, when, and why.

- Breathe: Create opportunities for you, your students, and the staff to breathe, literally and figuratively. Provide breathing exercises in class and pause the work for just a moment. Taking care of each other and our students is so important.

Try the 7, 7, and 7. Take a deep breath in for 7 seconds, hold it for 7 seconds, and breathe out slowly for 7 more seconds. This short, half-a-minute exercise can provide a moment of calm for all. Make it part of your routine, and see the benefits.

Provide Hope: Hope is an acronym. It stands for Hold On, Possibilities Exist. Let's be positive in our work for others in education and beyond. As I shared earlier with the story about the island where people did not have shoes, what is your mindset when you look at a situation? If you operate consistently with a positive lens, things will work out for you. Each situation we face as educators has multiple ways to manage and handle it. I believe it is a choice, a decision to be positive which provides hope for people. Not false hope—real, true belief that things will work out.

Look at these two statements: *There is nothing I can do* and *Let me see what I can do.* The first statement just shuts the door on any possibilities. Nothing? Really? There is nothing? You can't make a phone call, look a little deeper, try a different method, or bring in a second opinion? The second statement provides hope, and if it doesn't work out, at least you tried something. Providing hope for others is inspiring, energizing, and motivating. Keep at it. Keep being positive. Keep proving hope.

Putting on this HAT: Absorbing the chaos, creating calm, and providing hope. It touches all the bases on the very important work we are doing in schools and with our kids. These acts demonstrate care, leadership, wellness, and an authenticity that is so needed in our interactions with all we serve in schools. Stick these in your HAT as you lead in schools each day: staff, students, and parents.

🎩🎩🎩

It was an honor that you read our book, *HATS*. We—Jay, Andrew, and Brian—care deeply about educators and education. We want you to thrive and help those around you along the way. We need you. Those kids need you. Our future and our country *need you*.

We'll honorably borrow a line from the great Dr. Seuss to end our book.

> *Unless someone like you cares a whole awful lot,*
> *nothing is going to get better. It's not.*

We wish you the best on your journey. Keep rolling, friends. Keep bringing HATS to schools everywhere!

ABOUT THE AUTHORS

Jay Billy is the proud principal of Ben Franklin Elementary School in Lawrenceville, New Jersey. Jay is passionate about making school and learning fun and engaging for all, including all students, and creating a culture of creativity and curiosity. In 2016, Jay received the Exemplary Educator award from the New Jersey Dept. of Ed. He published his first book about school culture, called *Lead With Culture: What Really Matters in Our Schools*, published by Dave Burgess Consulting in 2018. Jay enjoys presenting at conferences and is passionate about school leadership and change.

In his personal life, Jay is the proud father of five children, Samantha, Michael, Delaney, Logan, and Fallon. As a former collegiate wrestling coach and high-school wrestling official, Jay enjoys going to the gym and keeping up with his fitness routines. In his professional life, Jay has been working in different capacities as part of Lawrence Township Public Schools since 2007 and has been in school leadership since 1997.

Andrew Marotta is an energetic and enthusiastic leader who has put his positive imprint on his beloved Port Jervis High School, in Port Jervis, New York. With the release of his first book, *The School Leader: Surviving and Thriving*, Andrew is expanding his impact on the educational-leadership community. Andrew is the author of five books, most recently completing this special project, *HATS: Heartfelt Acts for Teachers, Students, and Staff*.

In his personal life, Andrew is a loving husband to his wife, Jennifer, and a supportive father to their three young children, Claire, Matthew, and Tessa. In his professional life, Andrew has been leading at Port Jervis Schools in Port Jervis, New York, since 2005, serving as Assistant Principal for seven years and Principal for eleven. He has led the transformation of PJHS, helping to raise the graduation rate from the low 60% to almost 90%. After close to twenty years serving as a building leader, including most recently leading as Port Jervis Middle School Principal for two years, Andrew accepted a new role in Port Jervis Schools as the Director of Communications and Academic Services in the summer of 2023.

Andrew is a former men's Division 1 college basketball official, taking many leadership lessons from that time in his life to his leadership in schools and with school leaders. He lives and models the words on his logo: Energy, Enthusiasm, Extra, Effort, and Excellence!

Learn more at www.andrewmarotta.com and through his #ELBlog & #ELB podcast: Education Leadership & Beyond, found on Facebook, LinkedIn, Twitter @andrewmarotta21, and Instagram. #ELB #ELBlog, #survivethrive #keeprolling

He is grateful for his friendship and collaboration with Brian and Jay on this very special project. #HATS

Brian McCann recently finished his 18th year as principal of Joseph Case High School in Swansea, Massachusetts, from which he graduated in 1980. Brian has a bachelor's degree from Boston College in English and Speech-Theatre, a master's degree in journalism from the University of Michigan in Ann Arbor, and a CAGS from Fitchburg State University in Educational Leadership and Management.

He began teaching at his alma mater in 1989, taught English and Journalism for 11 years, and transitioned to high-school administration in 2000. Brian has contributed to NASSP's *Principal Leadership* magazine, prioritizing ed tech as a digital leader and the power of storytelling as a school administrator. He has also been a part of the recent compilation *100 No-Nonsense Things That ALL School Leaders Should STOP Doing* and the ed leadership book *The Principled Principal*. Brian is a passionate national speaker and loves to share his experiences in disrupting school-leadership norms, honing a positive school culture, and showcasing the community power of viral snow-day videos.

Brian recently celebrated his 30th wedding anniversary with his wife, Kathleen. They have three children: Fiona, Eliza, and Jack.

Brian McCann was Massachusetts' 2011 High School Principal of the Year and is one of NASSP's 2018 National Digital Principals of the Year. Look for him on Facebook, Instagram, LinkedIn, and Twitter.

Made in the USA
Middletown, DE
29 April 2024

53625490R00139